Water Bath Canning For The Beginner

Sumayyah .U Spencer

Introduction

Canning and preserving food is a time-honored tradition that allows us to enjoy the flavors of each season throughout the year. This cookbook serves as a guide for beginners, offering an overview of the essential techniques and recipes for water bath canning.

Before embarking on your canning and preserving journey, it's important to understand the basics. The overview of canning and preserving provided in this cookbook introduces you to the fundamentals of this age-old practice. You'll discover the importance of preserving food, not only for flavor but also for food security and sustainability.

To get started with water bath canning, you'll need the right gear. The chapter on canning and preserving gear outlines the essential equipment and tools required for safe and successful canning. From canners and jars to lids and utensils, this section will help you assemble everything you need for your canning adventures.

Water-bath canning is a simple and beginner-friendly method for preserving fruits, vegetables, and other low-acid foods. The cookbook delves into water-bath canning, explaining the process step by step. You'll learn how to prepare your ingredients, fill jars, create a proper seal, and process them in a water bath canner. With this knowledge, you'll be well-equipped to tackle a variety of recipes.

Ensuring the safety of your canned goods is paramount. The section on safe canning and preserving provides guidelines and best practices to prevent spoilage and foodborne illnesses. Following these safety tips is essential to enjoy your homemade preserves with confidence.

The heart of this cookbook lies in the recipes. From fruits to vegetables, you'll find a collection of mouthwatering recipes that showcase the flavors of the season. Whether you're preserving the sweetness of summer peaches or the savory goodness of garden-fresh tomatoes, these recipes guide you through the canning process with clear instructions and helpful tips.

Preserving isn't just about jams and jellies; it includes a range of delightful creations. The chapter on preserves, conserves, and some marmalades introduces you to different types of preserved foods, allowing you to explore diverse flavors and textures.

Salsas are a vibrant and versatile addition to your pantry. The cookbook includes a section dedicated to salsas, offering recipes that range from mild to spicy. These salsas can elevate your meals, adding a burst of flavor to everything from tacos to grilled chicken.

In conclusion, this book is your go-to resource for mastering the art of canning and preserving. Whether you're a newcomer or an experienced home cook, these pages provide the knowledge and inspiration to fill your pantry with delicious homemade creations that capture the essence of each season. Happy canning and preserving!

Contents

Chapter One Overview of Canning and Preserving

Canning and preserving as an art form has been less popular over the years as a result of our more fast-paced lives, the increased accessibility of refrigeration, and the proliferation of supermarkets. Many people began to see canning as more of a novelty activity, especially when it came to making preserves other than jams and jellies. However, there is a recent surge in the number of individuals interested in acquiring this skill. Because of the state of the economy, an increasing number of individuals are discovering that canning and other methods of food preservation provide a simple, low-cost option to stock their pantries.

This chapter will provide you with an overview of the four methods of canning and preserving that are discussed in this book. These methods are water-bath canning, pressure canning, freezing, and drying. Additionally, this chapter will explain the benefits, both practical and emotional, that canning and preserving your own foods can provide.

If you're new to canning and preserving, try not to let the restrictions overwhelm you or discourage you from getting started. This book provides clear, easy-to-follow instructions for each method that you may follow along with. Once you have a firm grasp of the fundamental steps involved in a technique, such as water-bath canning, it is time to turn your attention to the preparation of the dish you want to make.

Being Aware of the Numerous Advantages That Come With Canning and Preserving Your Own Food

Both canning and preserving food are methods that prevent food from going bad so that it may be consumed at a later date. Canning is one of the preservation techniques that was developed relatively recently in comparison to others, such as drying, which has been used since ancient times. One of life's true joys is having the ability to provide one's family and friends with meals that taste fresh and were either home-canned or preserved by oneself throughout the whole year. There is no question about this.

This book covers canning, freezing, and drying as methods for preserving food; nevertheless, the results of your efforts will be the same regardless of whatever technique you pick.

A larder brimming with items that have been recently harvested or prepared.

Having a well-stocked pantry provides a buffer against the ever-changing expense of purchasing nutritious meals. Canning food at home is a healthy and cost-effective method to preserve big or little amounts of high-quality food. If you appreciate the speciality foods from gourmet shops but despise the exorbitant costs, home canning is an option for you.

Convenience

It is possible to stock your pantry with items that are convenient to prepare, will appeal to your family, and will work with the active lifestyle you lead.

Belief in the quality of the components that make up your cuisine.

Canning and preserving food at home is the way to go if you are someone who places a high value on using fresh ingredients and want to maintain control over what goes into their meals.

A buffer against the effects of increasing food prices.

The purpose of canning and other methods of food preservation is to make use of fresh food in times when there is a plenty of it. And usually speaking, more food results in reduced prices.

A sense of relaxation and accomplishment.

For many people, working in the kitchen and handling food provides a sense of relaxation, and watching family and friends enjoy the products of one's efforts provides a great sense of accomplishment. Both of these feelings are derived from the experience of watching other people eat. It is rewarding and a source of pride for you, the home canner, to take the time to pick your recipe, choose and prepare your food, then package and process it so that it is safe.

A joyful experience.

The process of home-canning and preserving food is not only simple but also enjoyable, and who doesn't like having fun?

Over the course of the last several years, the cost of food has significantly increased. Everyone is concerned about the safety of the food they eat. Canning is the solution not just to the problem of high prices but also to the problem of providing healthy meals throughout the year. You will see an immediate return on your investment of time and energy into home-canning and preserving activities if you adhere to the recommended procedures for handling and preparing the food.

Canning and preserving food at home may have missed one or two generations, but one thing is certain: The practice is becoming more popular. Canning food at home is a skill that is practiced by both younger and older people of both sexes. It makes no difference whether you live in the city or in the country, even if you raise your own food; none of those factors are relevant anymore. Nearly each place you go can provide you with access to fresh food. Farmer's markets are becoming more frequent in many cities and towns, making it simple and convenient to locate the items that are ideal for preserving at prices that are reasonable.

Different sources provide somewhat different numbers when it comes to home canning, however Alltrista, the company that makes the most items for home canning, claims that around one in every four homes in the United States cans their own food. The majority of home-canned goods are consumed in the same households in which they are produced today. In addition, there are an increasing number of people who are devoted to eating locally, and the majority of these individuals are curious in the components of the foods that they consume. They are able to source the freshest food possible and have full control over the ingredients that go into their meals since they preserve it themselves.

Getting to Know Your Techniques: Preserving Food in Jars, Freezing It, and Drying It Out

When all of the stages for a method are followed, the methods that are covered in this book provide exceptional outcomes, making them suitable for usage in the comfort of one's own home. If you set your own regulations, you run the risk of lowering the standards for the quality and safety of the food you eat. One illustration of this would be cutting your processing time in half or failing to accurately time it. Both of these modifications might result in food becoming bad because the meal is not heated for a sufficient amount of time to kill all of the germs that are present in it.

Before you get started, make sure you've gone over the fundamental steps for the method of food preservation you'll be using. Even if you're already comfortable with the steps, it's a good idea to go over them once a year to jog your memory. During the process of preserving food, you will find that there are less interruptions. Always do a test run before to canning the food. This guarantees that you have all of the necessary materials and processes organized, allowing you to work swiftly and effectively.

After you have learned what each method accomplishes, which method is ideal for certain foods, the guidelines for the technique you pick, and safe food handling procedures, you will have no questions about your ability to prepare home-canned and -preserved foods in a manner that is safe for consumption. In the pages that follow, you will be given an introduction to both traditional and contemporary methods of canning and preserving food, both of which will make the process much simpler for you.

Regarding preserving food in jars.

The most widely utilized technique of food preservation in the modern era is canning. You should not believe anybody who tells you that home canning is difficult and dangerous. It's not even close to being true.

The preservation method known as canning involves subjecting food that has been hermetically sealed in a jar to heat in order to kill any germs that can cause the food to go bad. These microbes are found in every kind of food. Canning methods that are done correctly prevent food from going bad by applying heat to the food for a certain amount of time in order to eliminate harmful germs. In addition, when the jar cools and becomes sealed, the process of canning causes air to be expelled from the jar, which results in the creation of a vacuum. This inhibits the introduction of microbes, which would otherwise re-contaminate the food.

Approved procedures

Although you may hear of numerous different canning processes, the United States Department of Agriculture has only given its blessing to two of them (USDA). Canning in a water bath and canning under pressure are the two methods:

Canning in a water bath: A big kettle filled with boiling water is used in this technique, which is also referred to as hot water canning on occasion. Jars that have been filled are then heated to an internal temperature of 212 degrees for a certain amount of time while they are immersed in water. Utilize this approach for processing foods that are strong in acid, such as tomatoes, fruit, things produced from fruit, pickles, and anything that has been pickled.

Canning food under pressure.

Canning under pressure requires the use of a big kettle that generates steam inside of a sealed container. Under a specified pressure, measured with a dial gauge or weighted gauge that is located on the pressure-canner lid, the filled jars that are contained inside the kettle attain an interior temperature of 240 degrees Fahrenheit. This pressure is expressed in pounds. When processing vegetables and other items that are low in acid, such meat, poultry, and fish, you should use a canner that operates under pressure.

Don't get a pressure canner confused with a pressure cooker, which is a device that speeds up the cooking process. There is not enough space inside of a pressure cooker to accommodate both the canning jars and the water that is required to generate the appropriate level of pressure to properly preserve food.

Both the water-bath canning method and the pressure canning method involve heating the filled jars of food to a high temperature. This kills any microorganisms that may be present and creates a vacuum seal that is airtight. The only way to dependably make a safe product for canning is to utilize the technique that is appropriate for the kind of food you are preserving, follow the directions for your recipe to the letter, and finish all of the processing steps.

Avoid these canning processes at all costs.

The older canning techniques are not trustworthy, and as a result, they are not utilized, nor are they advised, for home canning in today's world. Occasionally, these techniques are "revived" as being quicker and easier than canning in a water bath or under pressure, however the use of any of the following methods is equivalent to playing Russian roulette with the safety of your food supply. Even if your grandmother may have used one of the following strategies, this does not in any way imply that it is secure for use today. Do yourself a favor and steer clear of any recipe that includes any of the following directions: "If you see instructions that require you to use any of the following methods, steer clear of that recipe."

Oven technique.

Jars that have been prepared in this manner are then put into a hot oven. This procedure is hazardous since it is quite unlikely that the interior temperature of your food will reach a high enough level to kill the germs and other bacteria that cause food to go bad. There is simply no assurance that the food contained in the jars will cook at the temperature that you have selected for your oven. Because of the abrupt drop in temperature that occurs when the oven door is opened, there is also a possibility that your jars may burst open.

Open-kettle approach.

The meal is prepared in an open saucepan and then placed in jars that have been sterilized in this technique. As the food cools, the two-piece lids are rapidly screwed on in the hopes of successfully sealing the jars. This technique results in a low vacuum seal on the jar, which has the potential to be ruptured when the jar fills with gas from spoiled food. This takes place because the bacteria in your meal are not killed by the heating process. There is also the possibility that your food can get infected when you are placing it in the jars to store it.

Method using steam.

A shallow pan that is covered and has a rack placed in the bottom is used for this procedure. When the pan containing the filled jars is put in the oven, steam will begin to move around the jars. This approach is dangerous because the jars are not heated uniformly and the steam is not pressured to get the food to a temperature high enough to kill any bacteria present in it. Canning under pressure is not to be confused with this procedure.

Oven with a microwave.

The temperature inside a microwave varies from model to model. As a result of this, it is impossible to establish criteria for processing periods that will produce a high temperature that will enter the jars and kill the germs that cause food to go bad.

Dishwasher.

Canning in a dishwasher is not recommended due to the fact that it is impossible to determine the precise temperature of each model of dishwasher and the temperature changes during the cycle of the cleaning process. It is not reliable enough to create a product that can be safely canned. On the other hand, you may use a dishwasher to clean your jars, and then you can leave them in the hot dishwasher while you prepare the contents of the jars.

Aspirin.

Don't laugh, but at one point in history, aspirin was employed in place of other methods of food preparation that included heat. Although it does include a germicidal agent that performs the function of a preservative, this agent does not kill the enzyme that is responsible for the degradation in food and the rotting of food.

Seal with wax or paraffin.

Once upon a time, people believed that sealing canned foods with wax or paraffin was a foolproof method. It has been shown that it cannot be relied upon. ... there is still the possibility that harmful botulism spores may form.

Pertaining to the freezing of food.

The process of freezing food involves preparing and packing foods while they are at their pinnacle of freshness and then placing them in the freezer to preserve all of the deliciousness that comes with the seasons. Freezing is an excellent approach for preserving foods that are incapable of withstanding the high heat and extended cooking times required by traditional methods of canning.

The three most important things to remember while freezing food are that it must be completely fresh, that it must be frozen as rapidly as possible, and that it must be maintained at an appropriate frozen temperature (0 degrees).

Simply placing anything in the freezer will not affect the quality to improve in any way. It is possible to avoid any reduction in the quality of food by wrapping it securely in freezer paper or storing it in freezer-safe containers. When your food comes into touch with the dry air inside of a freezer, it causes damage to the food. Food that has been harmed by the freezer may still be consumed, but it will have an unpleasant flavor. The freezer burn may be avoided by doing the following three things:

- Cut down on your time spent outside.
- Wrap the food in a tight package.
- Temperature swings should be avoided at all costs.

- Maintain the tightest seal you can on the freezer at all times.

- Before you open the door, you should have a plan for what you want to take out.

- Be careful not to overstuff your freezer. A freezer that is overstuffed restricts air circulation, which accelerates the rate of freezer deterioration.

Regarding the drying of food.

Drying food is the earliest technique of food preservation that has been discovered. When you dry food, you expose it to a temperature that is high enough to remove the moisture but low enough that it does not cook. This process removes the moisture from the food without cooking it. The food may be dried more uniformly with the help of good air circulation.

When it comes to drying, or "dehydrating," food, the best and most effective appliance to use is an electric dehydrator. The modern devices are equipped with a thermostat and a fan, which together contribute to much improved temperature regulation. You may also dry food by using the heat from your oven or the heat from the sun; however, the procedure will take longer and the results will be lower quality than food that has been dried using a dehydrator. Instructions for drying fruits, vegetables, and herbs may be found in Part V. Go there now.

Canning and preserving food successfully requires the following key skills.

The processes of canning and preserving food are not only straightforward and risk-free, but they also result in food that is not only wholesome but also delectable and completely satiating to the tongue. It requires time, effort, and familiarity with the proper procedures in order to become a good food preserver. Canning and preserving food at home may be accomplished with success if you follow these guidelines:

Begin with the most recent and greatest items that may be found. The quality of food is not improved by the process of preserving it. If you put trash in, you get rubbish out.

Before you begin your job, make sure you are familiar with the guidelines and procedures for the method of canning or preserving that you will be using. When you've already begun processing, it's too late to attempt to learn a new method.

Work should be broken up into short periods in order to avoid becoming fatigued and making errors.

Canning should be limited to one technique at a time, with no more than two different products being processed in a single day.

Keep yourself up to speed on any new or changed guidelines pertaining to your technique of preservation. This book is an excellent place to begin. You might also check out websites on the internet like as www.freshpreserving.com, which was developed by the people that produce Ball canning supplies. You may discover instructions and helpful hints for canning just about anything in this section.

For complete elimination of microorganisms, ensure that the appropriate processing technique and duration are used. The technique that you should use will be specified in the recipe; nevertheless, it is helpful to have an understanding of the distinction between high- and low-acid foods as well as the ways in which the canning processes for each kind of food vary.

Be aware of the altitude at which you are operating. When you are at an altitude that is more than 1,000 feet above sea level, you may need to adjust the processing time or the pressure.

Before you begin your session of preservation, make sure you have a strategy in place. Read your recipe (more than once). Make sure you have all of the necessary tools and supplies on hand to avoid running out at the last minute and having to take unscheduled breaks (make a list of what you need and check off items as you gather them).

Test your equipment. You need to do some tests on the equipment, whether you're using a pressure canner or an electric dehydrator, to make sure that everything is functioning as it should. In addition to that, you should constantly check the seals on your jars.

Make use of recipes that come from reputable sources or are ones that you have previously prepared successfully. Stick according to the instructions given in the recipe. You should not alter the proportions, swap out the components, or come up with your own unique culinary combinations. It is impossible to preserve food safely while also relying on improvisation. Because of this, it is not possible to double the recipe. If the amount that the recipe produces is not enough for your needs, you may always prepare another batch. Always be sure to use jars of the correct size, which may be found in the recipe. It is possible that the yield and the end outcome will be affected if you try to use a jar that is either bigger or smaller.

At this point in the food preservation procedure, you are prepared to transport your food to its ultimate location. You may preserve food by canning it, freezing it, or drying it. Whichever method you select, move confidently along the path of canning and preserving.

Chapter Two
Canning and Preserving Gear

How often have you been exposed to the adage "Use the right tool for the job"? When it comes to preserving and canning food, this adage could not be more accurate. The bulk of the goods that are covered in this chapter won't put a dent in your cash account, but they will make the canning and preserving jobs that you do more effective. When you prepare your fresh ingredients in a shorter amount of time, the end result will have higher quality and a more robust taste.

This chapter provides a rundown of the instruments and implements that you will need in order to successfully carry out your responsibilities. Canning is the sole use for many implements, such as jar lifters and lid wands. Other implements, such as cooking utensils and knives, are used on a daily basis for a variety of jobs throughout the year. Invest in tools and equipment of a high grade since the value you get out of their quality and longevity will more than cover the cost of the investment.

Assorted Primitive Equipment.

The majority of the equipment that is required for canning and preserving food is standard fare and may be found in kitchens that are well equipped. When a tool for canning is recommended in a recipe, it is because there is a good justification for using that instrument. When the appropriate equipment is used for the task at hand, there is less of a possibility that a jar will not seal well or will be able to retain germs. It may also lessen the likelihood of accidents and injuries occurring.

Important and fundamental implements and implements.

These fundamental implements are required for every kind of job done in the kitchen that takes it seriously. Buy items of the highest quality that your budget will allow. Things of high quality will continue to look great even as you get older.

Knives.

You can get by with only three knives: a paring knife, a multipurpose knife with a blade measuring 6 inches, and a chef's knife measuring 8 inches (although some people prefer a chef's knife measuring 10 inches). When shopping for excellent knives, there are two types of blades you should look for: stamped or forged blades, and blades composed of high carbon steel or stainless steel (tempered steel knives are no longer the epitome of high quality cutlery). Ceramic is another another material that produces high-quality blades, but unlike its rivals made of steel, ceramic knives are more susceptible to being damaged. Additionally, if you choose knives that are well-balanced, the knife will perform the job for you rather than requiring your assistance.

Taking the necessary steps to maintain your knives will safeguard your financial investment. Always make sure your blades are razor sharp. Keep them from coming into contact with one another by storing them in a block or on a magnetic strip designed for storing knives. Wash them by hand (dishwashers are notorious for being hard on dishes, and knives take the brunt of banging around with the other silverware).

Cups used for measuring.

When it comes to canning, it is very necessary to measure the ingredients with extreme precision in order to produce the ideal proportions of each component. There are measuring cups designed specifically for dry components, such as flour, sugar, and solid fats; and there are measuring cups designed specifically for liquid ingredients, such as water, milk, and other beverages.

Glass, plastic, or metal are the common materials used in the construction of measuring cups for liquids. When using glass measuring cups, the quantity of liquid that is contained in the cup may be plainly seen.

Spoons used for measuring.

These are available in a range of sizes, from an eighth of a teaspoon to two tablespoons. Canning foods requires precise measurements, so avoid using adjustable measuring spoons. These spoons are prone to shifting, which might result in inaccurate readings.

If you want to avoid having to stop what you're doing and clean your measuring spoons every time you measure the same quantity of wet and dry components, have two sets of measuring spoons on hand: one set for dry ingredients and one set for wet ones.

Spoons.

You will need at least a pair of cooking spoons made of a metal that does not react with food, such as stainless steel. These spoons should not alter the flavor of foods that are acidic when they come into touch with them. Stainless steel, anodized aluminum, glass, and enameled cast iron are all examples of nonreactive metals. Other options include. You might also use a selection of wooden spoons ranging in size from little to large.

Rubber spatulas.

These may be purchased in a wide range of hues and dimensions, ranging from flat to spoon-shaped forms. When you are preparing foods that contain sugar, use ones that are resistant to heat. Check to see that the head does not readily detach from the handle, since this is a regular issue with spatulas that are less costly.

Tongs.

Tongs are in helpful for a wide variety of tasks in the kitchen, but they are particularly useful for transferring big portions of food into and out of boiling water. Experiment with the spring-loaded type available in a range of lengths. It is important not to miss the locking mechanism. When not in use, the tongs will remain closed thanks to this feature.

Ladle.

Utilize a ladle that can withstand high temperatures and has an effective pouring spout.

Potholders.

Keep your hands away from anything that might become hot. Always have twice as many potholders on hand as you believe you'll need in a given situation.

When canning, potholders often get soaked with water. Keep a sufficient supply on hand so that you won't have to resort to using damp potholders. A serious burn may result from the rapid transfer of heat that takes place via a wet potholder in the form of steam.

Towels for the kitchen and paper towels also.

You may use them to wipe the rims of your jars and as a cushion for them while they are cooling.

Graters.

You have at least four different choices for shredding and grating when you use a box grater. An upgraded form of a tool used for dealing with wood called a rasp, a microplane grater is ideal for extracting the zest off citrus fruits like lemons and limes.

Zester.

Before the invention of the microplane grater, the equipment used to remove the zest from citrus fruits was called a zester (just the skin without the bitter white part). However, if you need a greater quantity of zest (at least a teaspoon), you should use a microplane grater rather than this tool since it is more efficient for smaller quantities.

Scissors.

Instead of using blades, cutting open food packaging with scissors is safer. If you wash your scissors after cutting meat, you may prevent the spread of germs from one cut to the next.

Timer.

Pick a timer that is simple to read, uncomplicated to program, and loud enough that you can hear it even if you leave the room. Think about obtaining two of these to guarantee accuracy.

Waterproof pens and markers.

Choose ones that won't come off easily.

Labels.

You may create labels out of masking tape or freezer tape, personalize your own labels using your home computer, or purchase modest numbers of labels from a firm such as My Own Labels.

Board for cutting on.

A quality cutting board will not only keep your blades safe but also provide you with a work area that can be moved around.

A thermometer for candy.

An accurate reading of the temperature of candy and sugar may be obtained with a candy thermometer. It is used in the canning process to monitor the temperature of the food that has been prepared. Some candy thermometers contain markings that indicate the moment at which jelly reaches its gel stage (220 degrees). Invest in a candy thermometer that has a base to support it and is simple to read. This will ensure that the bulb section of the thermometer does not come into contact with the bottom of your pan. In this scenario, the readout of the temperature on your thermometer will not be correct. Many of them come equipped with a clip that may be used to protect the bulb from touching the base.

If you have the space available, keep a second thermometer in a convenient area. You will have a backup in the event that you accidently damage one while you are canning.

The following things are not required in every circumstance, but it would be beneficial to have them. If you don't currently have any of these things in your kitchen, you should start collecting them as you discover you need them. They don't take up a lot of space, but you'll find yourself reaching for them whenever you have the chance because of how useful they are.

Vegetable peeler.

Carrots, potatoes, and apples may all be peeled using this device.

Masher for potatoes.

Crushing your cooked veggies or fruits in this manner is a breeze thanks to this tool.

Lemon juicer.

You can quickly extract the juice from any citrus fruit with this gadget, which is compatible with all citrus fruits. Simply split the fruit in half, place the tip of the juicer into one side of the fruit, and start pressing.

Squeezing your fruit into a mesh strainer that is sitting on the side of a measuring cup allows you to measure your juice while simultaneously removing the pulp and seeds from the fruit.

Melon baller.

You can quickly and simply remove the seeds from a cucumber that has been cut in half by using a melon baller. This will prevent the seeds from flying all over your kitchen.

Corer.

This device is able to extract apple cores without causing any damage to the fruit. When you're dealing with pounds of apples, this is a fantastic way to save time.

Pitter for cherries and olives.

There is no other method that is more effective for extracting cherry and olive pits. Purchase the size of pitter that can accommodate the fruit you want to pit.

A variety of cookware, including pots, pans, and mixing bowls.

You probably already have a variety of saucepans, skillets, and bowls to use for combining ingredients. In such case, you shouldn't worry since you don't have to make all of your purchases at once. You should begin with a solid base collection, and then add pieces to it as you discover more uses for them.

Pots.

Pots are deep, ranging in size from 5 to 8 quarts, feature two looped handles (one on each side of the pot), and provide adequate area for the growth of food during a vigorous rolling boil. When cooking jams, jellies, or other condiments that need consistent heat distribution, a pot of high quality and with a hefty bottom is required.

Saucepans.

The capacity of saucepans may vary anywhere from one to three quarts. They often include a cover that is custom-made to suit the pan and have a lengthy grip on one side of the pan.

Bowls for mixing.

Maintain a selection of different sized mixing bowls in your kitchen. Look for sets that come in several sizes and can be stacked inside each other for convenient storage.

The most long-lasting bowls are those that are crafted from glass and stainless steel.

Invest in bowls for mixing that have level bottoms rather than rounded ones. They will not move around all over the kitchen counter while you are working with them. Put a moist dishtowel beneath the bowl and aggressively stir it while the cloth is in place. This keeps the bowl, once it has been filled, from slipping.

Colander.

Colanders aren't simply for draining spaghetti. They are ideal for rinsing and draining many types of produce, particularly fruits and vegetables. Put the food in your colander, and then place it inside of a sink that is completely full of water. Take the colander out of the water, and while you concentrate on other things, let the food to drain in the colander.

Wire basket.

Blanching is a breeze when done using a wire or mesh basket that can be collapsed and has a lifting handle. Put the food that is in the basket into the water that is already boiling in the pot. When the allotted time for blanching has passed, remove the food-filled basket from the water that is boiling.

Specialized tools that simplify and expedite the task.

The canning tasks that you need to complete absolutely need every item on this list. They will all save you a significant amount of time.

Prepared food machine.

- Invest in a food processor of the highest possible quality that you can afford.
- It has to be weighty and solidly constructed so that it does not move about on your kitchen counter while the processing is taking place.

Food mill.

Fruits and vegetables may be puréed in a food grinder, which also removes the skin and any seeds. To do this, you will need to manually crank the blade, which will cause the pulp to be forced into the mill. You should look for a food mill that sits on the edge of your bowl or pot. This will allow you to use one hand to support the mill while using the other hand to turn the blade of the mill.

Blender.

You may quickly purée fruits and vegetables using a blender, but before you do so, you must first remove the skin and any seeds. It is important to avoid introducing an excessive amount of air into your diet.

A scale for food.

When your canning recipe calls for specific amounts of fruit or vegetables based on their weight, you will need a food scale. Spring and electronic scales are the two most prevalent kinds of food scales used today.

When you have a food scale that is marked in metric quantities, converting the components in a recipe is a simple.

Before weighing your food, you may use a spring scale, which is often referred to as a manual scale. This kind of scale enables you to put a bowl on top of the scale and manually change the weight setting until it reads 0. After you have put your meal on the scale, you may determine its weight by reading the indication that is located on the dial.

A digital display may be found on an electronic scale that is powered by a battery. The price is more than that of a spring scale, but it is simpler to use. Try to find one that includes a tare function. If you use a bowl to contain your meal, you will be able to add zero pounds to the scale thanks to this feature. If you have the option, go for an electronic or digital scale. They are more accurate.

Machines for creating vacuum seals: When it comes to eliminating air from food storage bags, the piece of equipment that is the most effective is a vacuum sealer. When packaging dry goods or preserving raw or cooked items in the freezer, vacuum sealers are an invaluable tool to have. Once you have one, you will understand the full worth of it, despite the fact that it takes up space and may be expensive. Hand-held vacuum sealers are a recent addition to the consumer goods industry. When compared to the cost of acquiring an electric model, they might be a more affordable choice.

Canning Equipment.

Because the equipment in this area has been developed specifically for canning, it is likely that you will only make use of it during the canning season and not very often outside of that time. Make sure that you keep these things in a place that is well-kept and secure. In addition, make it a habit to inspect each component for signs of wear and tear after each time it is used.

Canning vessels.

Canning necessitates the use of either a pressure canner or a water-bath canner, the distinction between the two being based on the sort of food that will be preserved.

Canning pot with a water bath.

A water-bath canner, also known as a boiling-water canner, is a kind of kettle that is used for the preparation of foods that are high in acidity (primarily fruits, jams, jellies, condiments, and pickled foods). The canner is a huge pot made of enamelware or stainless steel that has a cover that is designed to fit snugly and a rack for holding jars.

Pressure canner.

A pressure canner, also known as a steam-pressure canner, is a device that seals low-acid foods (mainly vegetables, meats, fish, and poultry) inside of an airtight container while applying a predetermined amount of pressure to the contents of that container. The pressure of the steam within the canner can be measured using either a weighted gauge or a dial gauge. This guarantees that the high temperature of 240 degrees will be reached in order to treat your food in a sanitary manner.

Equipment for canning.

Canning food in a water bath or under pressure requires the use of these essential instruments. In the kitchen, safety should always come first, and having the appropriate tools for safely handling hot, **full jars and other heavy pieces of canning equipment is very necessary.**

Jar lifter.

A jar lifter is an essential piece of equipment that you should never be without. It is the most effective tool that you may use to move hot canning jars into and out of your canning kettle as well as your pressure canner. This peculiar-looking gadget, which is rubberized and shaped like tongs grips the jar by its neck (the region immediately below the threaded section at the top of the jar), preventing the screw band from being disturbed in the process.

Foam skimmer

The use of a foam skimmer makes it simple to remove foam from the surface of hot jelly, jam, or marmalade while allowing any fragments of fruit or rind to remain in the liquid. (The apertures of slotted spoons are much too big to allow for the removal of foam in a rapid and effective manner.)

Jars for use in home canning.

Home canning has evolved over the years to include a wide variety of jars and seals suitable for preserving food at home. Mason jars are another term for the widely used jars that carry the labels Ball and Kerr. Mason jars are the most prevalent kind of jar. After the heat treatment, a vacuum seal is created in the jar by using a cap that consists of two separate pieces.

Use only jars that have been specifically certified for home canning and are constructed of tempered glass today to keep your home-canned food safe. Glass may be "tempered," which is a treatment technique that makes it resistant to breaking at high temperatures. This makes it possible for jars to be processed in canners that reach temperatures as high as 212 degrees Fahrenheit (or 240 degrees Fahrenheit) without cracking.

Jars for home canning are available in a variety of sizes, including 4 ounce, 1/2 pint, 12 ounce, 1 pint, and 1 quart. Both a regular-mouth and a wide-mouth option are available, with the former being about 2 1/2 inches in diameter and the latter measuring approximately 3 1/8 inches in diameter. Jars with a regular mouth are the ones that are most often used for storing jelly, jam, relish, or any other kind of cooked food. Canning vegetables, pickles, and meats are the most common uses for jars with wide mouths since it is simpler to place big portions of food within the broad hole. Wide-mouth jars are also often used for storing dry goods.

Two-piece caps.

The screw band and the lid that make up a two-piece cap are both made of metal. They are designed to work only with the jars used in contemporary home canning processes.

Lids.

When it is heated, the rubber-like component that serves as a sealing compound on the underneath edge of the lid becomes more pliable. After the time of heat processing, this compound forms a seal that is impermeable to air by adhering to the rim of a jar that has been well cleaned. Lids aren't reusable.

Turn band screws.

The screw band has two purposes: it keeps the lid in place while the jar is being processed, and it also keeps the lid in place after the jar has been opened and is being stored in the refrigerator. Before you store the canned food, you must first ensure that the jars have effectively sealed by checking them once they have cooled and then remove the screw band.

As long as there are no traces of corrosion or rust on the screw bands, and as long as they have not been bent or dented, they may be used several times.

Mason jars

Why are they referred to as Mason jars yet the brands Ball and Kerr make the glass jars that are used for home canning the most often? James Landis Mason, the man who invented the Mason jar, gave it his namesake. He came up with the idea for and went on to patent a one-of-a-kind glass jar that has a lid that can be screwed on and creates an airtight seal for food. The big stoneware pots that had been used in the past for storing food have been replaced by this jar that can be easily sealed.

After World War II, the tapered jars that are still in use today were first manufactured. They employ a two-part cap, which consists of a lid and a metal screw band that can be screwed into the threaded top of the jar. These days, the term "Mason jar" refers, more or less, to any and all jars used for home canning. I would want to express my gratitude to Mr. Mason for simplifying the process of home-canning by using screw-top closures.

Lid wand.

A magnet is attached to one end of a heat-resistant stick on the end of a lid wand. Using it, you may remove a lid from boiling water and position it on the rim of a full jar without contacting the lid or causing the sealing compound to become disrupted.

If you want to keep your lids from becoming stuck together in the boiling water in your pan, you should stack them such that the tops are touching and the undersides are touching. If they do end up sticking together, you may separate them by dipping them into a basin filled with cold water. Before you use them, give them a quick rewarming in the hot water for a few seconds. You should also tilt the lids slightly when you put them in the water. Because of this, they remain spread out and are much simpler to pick up one at a time.

A spatula made of thin plastic.

The best instrument for removing air bubbles from between the bits of food that are packed into your filled jars is a plastic spatula that is thin and flexible. Rather of spending a lot of money on utensils, consider picking up a set of chopsticks instead. Do not use a metal item or a bigger object for this task, since doing so may taint your meal and cause the heated jar to shatter or break.

Canning funnel with a wide aperture.

You are able to swiftly and cleanly fill your canning jars by using a wide-mouth funnel, which is designed to fit into the inner edge of either a regular- or wide-mouth canning jar. Canning relies heavily on this particular piece of equipment.

The use of a strainer or a jelly bag

In order to extract juice from cooked fruit in preparation for creating jelly, a jelly bag is constructed. It won't break the bank to buy one of these bags, but if you'd rather create your own, you can line a metal strainer with cheesecloth and use it as a substitute. Make use of a strainer that is suspended on the side of your cooking pot or mixing bowl so that it does not come into contact with the liquid.

Crocks made of stoneware.

Stoneware crocks are often sold without lids and are available in capacities ranging from 1 gallon to 5 gallons. They do not react with other substances and are used in the production of olives and pickles. Make sure that you only use crocks that have a glazed inside and are certified to be free of lead and cadmium. Cadmium is a kind of zinc ore that is used in the production of paints and colors.

When utilizing stoneware crocks that have been previously used, use caution. The coating on these crocks often included lead, which may contaminate anything you store inside of them. This is an item that is better off being acquired brand new rather than used due to the fact that the history of used things may frequently not be determined.

Instruments and Gadgets Necessary for the Freezing of Food

You probably already have in your kitchen some of the ingredients and equipment needed to preserve food using this simple method.

A freezer.

The freezer that is connected to your refrigerator is typically of a size that is enough for freezing food. On the other hand, if you plan on preserving a significant quantity of food, you should consider purchasing a separate freezer unit.

Containers that are rigid.

Glass or plastic may be used to construct them. Make sure you only use containers that are suitable for the freezing conditions of a freezer. In order to prevent the accumulation of smells and dry air in the freezer, plastic containers should be nonporous and of sufficient thickness. Glass containers need to be prepared so that they can withstand the low temperatures of a freezer, and they also need to be robust enough to prevent splitting when subjected to the pressure of expanding food while the food is frozen.

Freezer bags.

Make sure you're using freezer-safe bags that come in appropriate dimensions for the quantity of food you have.

Wrapping paper and freezer paper: Your food will be protected against freezer burn, which occurs when air comes into touch with your food while it is stored in the freezer. This laminated paper will do the trick. Use this paper as a tape to ensure that the wrap remains securely closed. One other excellent option for wrapping frozen foods is heavy-duty aluminum foil, which does not need to be taped.

Wrap food products in aluminum foil and then put them inside a freezer bag to provide further protection against freezer damage.

Instruments and Appliances Required for Drying Food

The process of eliminating moisture from food by dehydration is a time-consuming and laborious one that requires the food to be heated at a low temperature. In order to complete this procedure successfully, you will need the following things.

An electric dehydrator.

Your food is dried in an enclosed room by this machine, which also surrounds the chamber with warm air and circulates it.

A typical oven.

Use your oven to dry food before purchasing an electric food dehydrator if it has a low temperature setting and you can do without it for up to 24 hours. This will save you money.

Oven thermometer.

You may determine if the temperature in your oven is low enough to dry your food without also cooking it with the use of an oven thermometer.

Stackable trays and racks

These are used to hold your food while it is drying, and they come in a variety of sizes.

They are provided at no additional cost with an electric dehydrator. When drying things in an oven, use baking sheets or frames covered with mesh. When drying food in the sun, clean screens and cheesecloth are required to keep insects away from the food as it dries and to prevent the food from spoiling.

Chapter Three
Water-bath Canning

Canning food in a water bath involves bringing jars that have been filled with food to a boil in a pot that is specifically designed for the purpose. Fruits and tomatoes are two of the most common items that are canned using the water-bath method. Other foods that are often canned using this method include jams, jellies, marmalades, chutneys, relishes, pickled vegetables, and other condiments.

Canning food in a water bath may make you worry whether this method is risky to use when preserving food at home. Rest assured that the answer is an unequivocal "Yes!" as long as the directions and rules for safe canning are adhered to. In this chapter, you will learn which items may be canned without risk using a water-bath canner, as well as get detailed instructions on how to successfully complete the canning process. In no time at all, you will be able to amaze and satiate your loved ones by producing sparkling jars full of delicious home-cooked treats for them to enjoy.

Water-bath The Basics of Preserving Food in Jars

Canning food in a water bath, sometimes known as the boiling-water technique, is the simplest and easiest way to preserve high-acid food, most often fruit, tomatoes, and pickled vegetables. Canning food in a water bath is frequently referred to as the boiling-water method.

You can preserve food using the water-bath canning method by placing the prepared jars in a water-bath canner, which is a kettle specifically designed for this method of canning (for more information on the canner and other necessary equipment, see the section titled "Key equipment for water-bath canning"); bringing the water to a boil; and then maintaining that boil for a certain number of minutes, which is determined by the type of food and the size of the jar Maintaining a temperature of 212 degrees Fahrenheit in the water requires that you keep the water boiling in the jar-filled kettle during the processing duration. It is essential to maintain this temperature in order to prevent the growth of mold, yeast, enzymes, and bacteria in foods with a high acid content.

Canning food in a water bath is one of the two ways that are advised for canning food at home safely. Even though each processing method employs a distinct piece of machinery and set of procedures, the end aim is the same: to kill any living germs and microbes that may be present in your food so that it may be consumed at a later time without risk. This is performed by bringing the food that is contained inside the jars to a higher temperature and then forming a vacuum seal.

The water-bath canning method and the pressure-canning method are not interchangeable because the temperature that can be reached in a water bath only reaches 212 degrees, while the temperature that can be reached in a pressure canner reaches 240 degrees. This temperature difference is necessary to ensure that low-acid foods are processed in a safe manner.

Foods that can be safely canned after being submerged in water.

Only high-acid foods, defined as those with a pH factor (the measure of acidity) of 4.6 or below, may be successfully water-bathe canned in a water bath. So, what exactly is a meal that is rich in acid? One of the following two options:

Foods that naturally contain a lot of acid include:

These foods comprise the majority of fruits.

Foods that already have a low acid content but may be made more acidic by the addition of another acid. The fact that pickled vegetables are included in this category demonstrates that it is safe to can them in a water bath. By adding an acid to foods that are naturally low in acid, such as vinegar, lemon juice, or citric acid, a white powder that is derived from the juice of acidic fruits such as lemons, limes, and pineapples, the degree of acidity in the meal may be altered. Pickles produced from cucumbers, relish prepared from zucchini or summer squash, and green beans seasoned with dill are a few examples of foods that have been changed to have lower levels of acid. These days, most people consider tomatoes to be part of this group. They can be processed in a water-bath canner, but for reasons of food safety, you must first add some kind of acid to them.

Don't take a guess if your recipe doesn't inform you whether technique of processing (water-bath canning or pressure canning) is best for your product. Instead, follow the instructions in the recipe.

Instead, you should use litmus paper to determine the pH level of the meal you are consuming. If the pH of your food is 4.6 or below, you should can it using the water-bath technique; if the pH of your food is 4.7 or higher, you should can it using the pressure-cooking method.

Essential components for the process of water-bath canning.

When you are doing your own home canning, you don't want to make mistakes like changing the proportions of the components in a recipe or skipping a stage in the canning process. You also don't want to use the improper equipment. Because you have this equipment, you will be able to securely process and handle your filled jars.

The cost of the equipment used for canning in a water bath is much lower than the cost of the equipment used for canning under pressure. Canning kettles with water baths range anywhere from $25 to $45 in price. You may be able to find a "starter kit" for approximately $50 to $60 that contains the canning kettle, the jar rack, a jar lifter, a wide-mouth funnel, and jars all in one convenient package. This could be the case.

For canning in a water bath to be done in a safe and effective manner, the following is a list of the equipment that you must have on hand at all times, without exception or substitution:

A canner that uses a water bath.

The water-bath canner is comprised of a large kettle that is often constructed of porcelain-coated steel or aluminum. It has a lid that is custom-built to suit the kettle, a capacity of up to 21 to 22 quarts of water, and employs a rack to hold the jars (for more information, see the next item). You cannot use a big stock pot in place of a canner that uses a water bath. It is crucial for the jars to be sitting off the bottom of the canner, and the canner set comes with racks that are designed to fulfill this function.

Aluminum is a reactive metal, which means that it imparts its flavor to food that comes into direct contact with it. However, aluminum can be used in a water-bath canner even though the food will not come into direct contact with the aluminum. This is because the food will be contained within a sealed jar.

A jar rack.

Canners that use a water bath often include a jar rack attached to the bottom of the canning kettle. This rack is typically made of stainless steel and is designed to hold canning jars. During the time that the jars are being processed in the water bath, it prevents the jars from colliding with one other or the bottom of the kettle, while also keeping the jars in an upright position. You are able to securely move your filled jars into and out of your canning kettle thanks to the rack's lifting handles, which enable you to hang it on the inner edge of the kettle.

Canning jars.

For home canning, the only kind of jars that are suggested to use are canning jars. Make sure you use the jar size that is specified in your recipe.

Two-piece caps (lids and screw bands).

After the jar has been processed in the water bath, the lids and screw bands are used to establish a vacuum seal that will keep the contents of the jar fresh and ready for use at a later time. This seal prevents bacteria from getting back into your food once they have been removed.

Rubber rings of the older design are not advised for use any more. The reliability of the seal is no longer sufficient for it to result in a product that is risk-free, despite the fact that some used ones may still be accessible. These rubber rings are available at select establishments that specialize in canning; but, as a result of their uniqueness, they are very expensive and only available in very limited numbers. Canning food for a family's pantry should not be done in jars with such a whimsical design; rather, save them for giving as delightful food presents.

In addition to the things that are a must-have, which were just stated, you could also desire the things that are listed below. Even if the results of your job won't be affected by the following components, using them will allow you to complete your tasks in a more organized and time-saving manner:

- A teapot or saucepan that is pre-heated to boiling and may be used as a reserve supply of water.

- A funnel with a broad opening and a ladle, which will make it much simpler to put food into jars. In order to facilitate a better seal, the funnel also ensures that the rims of the jars remain clean.

- A lid wand, which allows you to move lids from boiling water to jars without touching them, and a jar lifter, which allows you to move canning jars into and out of your canning kettle without risking injury. Both of these tools are available at most home improvement stores.

- A flexible plastic spatula on the end of which air bubbles may be pushed out of the jar.

The path that leads to the completion of your project.

It is imperative that you do not omit any step of the canning process, regardless of how unimportant you may believe that particular step to be. You will be able to produce a securely processed product that can be used at a later time when your food preservation methods are in perfect harmony and balance with one another.

The steps involved in making delectable, handmade delights of superior quality for your loved ones are broken down into the following parts of this article for your perusal and reference.

Always observe correct procedures for sanitation and cleanliness in the kitchen, handle food with care, and strictly adhere to the instructions provided in the recipe. Make no changes to the recipe, and don't skip any of the processing steps.

The first thing you need to do is prepare your gear.

When you begin the process of canning, the first thing you do is examine all of your supplies and have everything ready so that when you are through preparing the food (which is Step 2 of the canning process), you can immediately begin filling your jars.

Check the jars, lids, and screw bands that you have.

Always be sure to read the directions provided by the manufacturer before preparing your jars, lids, and screw bands. The following are some things to look for while inspecting your jars, lids, and screw bands for any defects:

Jars.

You should inspect the jar edges for any nicks, chips, or cracks in the glass, and throw away any jars that have any of these flaws. If you want to reuse jars, first remove any stains or remnants of food that may be on them, and then inspect each one carefully for any flaws.

Turn band screws.

Check to see whether the bands have become misshapen, corroded, or rusted.

In order to determine whether or not the band is circular, screw it onto a jar. It may be used if the process of tightening it down is easy and doesn't encounter any resistance. Throw away any bands that are damaged in any way or are not perfectly round (bent or not completely round).

As long as the screw bands remain in excellent condition, they may be used again without losing their original shape. In addition, since you remove the bands after the jars have cooled, you won't need as many of them as you would for the jars.

Lids.

All of the lids have to be brand new. Lids aren't reusable. It is important to ensure that the sealant on the bottom of each lid is equal. Do not use lids that are damaged or scraped in any way.

Incorrect lids will prevent a vacuum seal from being created. Do not purchase used lids from thrift stores or antique shops. Older lids will not form a good seal when used.

Clean your jars, as well as their lids and screw bands.

After checking the jars for nicks or chips, the screw bands for appropriate fit and corrosion, and the new lids for defects and scratches, wash everything in warm, soapy water, being sure to thoroughly rinse the goods and get rid of any soap residue that may have been left behind. Throw away any products that are broken or not up to standard.

Start heating the water in the kettle.

Start by filling your canning kettle with water to a level that is between one-half and two-thirds full, then bring the water to a simmer. Keep in mind that the water level will significantly increase when you add the jars that are already full. At this stage, you want to avoid filling it up too much.

Warm up some more water in a saucepan or teakettle to use as a reserve. A minimum of one to two inches of water need to be present in each of the jars before you proceed with the process. You may skip the step of waiting for the whole canner to reheat before proceeding if you add water that has already been heated.

Maintaining the temperature of your equipment and jars while you wait for them to be filled.

During the time that you are waiting for your jars to be filled, you should immerse the jars and lids in hot water (not boiling water), and you should maintain your screw bands clean and handy in the following manner:

Jars.

Put them in your tea kettle and fill it with boiling water. Let them sit there for at least ten minutes. Maintain them in that location until you are prepared to fill them.

Lids.

They should be submerged in water that is hot but not boiling in a saucepan. The lid sealant may be preserved by removing them from the jars and storing them in a separate location.

Turn band screws.

These do not need being maintained at a very high temperature, but they must be kept clean. Put them in the area where you're going to be filling the jars.

The second step is to prepare your meal.

When you are preserving food, you should only ever utilize the most best ingredients. You won't be able to achieve the level of quality in your finished product that you want if you accept anything less than the very finest. Sort through your food with care, throwing away any items that are damaged in any way or that you would not consume in its raw condition.

Prepare your meal in accordance with the directions provided in the recipe, such as stripping it of its skin or peel and chopping it into little pieces.

In a similar vein, be sure to cook your meal in accordance with the instructions provided in the recipe. You must not alter the amounts of the components or the ingredients themselves in any way. Any modification may result in a change in the acidity of the product, which would necessitate the use of pressure canning rather than canning in a water bath in order to destroy microorganisms.

When a recipe calls for a certain ingredient or step, there is a good rationale for include it. If you don't follow the directions for the recipe to the letter, the end product won't be what the recipe was aiming for in the first place.

Step 3: Filling your jars.

- As soon as the jars you have prepared are ready, add the food you have prepared (whether it is cooked or raw) together with the hot liquid. Proceed in the following manner:

- Move the prepared food into the heated jars, adding the hot liquid or syrup if the recipe asks for it, and making sure there is enough headspace left over.

- To swiftly fill your jars, you should make use of a funnel with a large opening and a ladle. This will prevent a significant amount of spillage, as well as reduce the amount of residue that accumulates on the rims of your jars. Before you fill your jars, placing them on a clean kitchen towel will not only make cleaning easier but will also save you from sliding.

- Use a spatula or another implement made of a material other than metal to pop any air bubbles that may have formed. After removing the air bubbles, you will need to replenish the prepared food or liquid in the jar in order to retain the appropriate headspace.

- Always be sure to remove any air bubbles and leave the amount of headspace that is indicated in your recipe before attaching the two-piece caps. The creation of a vacuum seal and the preservation of your food both need you to complete these processes.

- Use a fresh, wet towel to wipe the rims of the jars.

- If there is even a particle of food on the rim of the jar, the sealant on the edge of the lid will not make contact with the rim, and the jar will not be able to be sealed.

- Hand-tighten the screw band after placing a heated lid on each jar's rim with the sealant side making contact with the rim of the jar.

- Be careful not to overtighten since the process of sealing requires some space for air to escape.

Step 4: Process your jars once they have been filled.

Now that your jars are full, you may start the processing step of the recipe. Proceed in the following manner:

- Put the jar rack in the canning kettle and suspend it so that the handles hang over the inner rim of the pot.

- When placing the full jars on the jar rack, take care to ensure that they remain upright and do not come into contact with one another.

- Even if the capacity of your kettle seems to be rather enormous, resist the urge to cram as many jars as possible into the canner. Place only as many jars as can be done so without restricting the flow of water from one to the next while still having enough room. And remember to only ever process jars on the jar rack in a single layer at a time.

- You should never process half-pint or pint jars with quart jars because the increased volume of food in quart jars needs a longer processing period to destroy any germs and microbes that could be present. You may process jars of the half-pint and pint sizes together if your recipe asks for the same amount of processing time for each of those sizes.

- Remove the hook that secures the jar rack to the side of the kettle, then gently drop it into the boiling water. If more water is required, add it at this point.

- It is very natural for air bubbles to emerge from the jars. If the water in your jars does not reach a depth of at least 1 inch, use some of the boiling water that you have set aside. To keep from scalding yourself with hot water, take cautious to pour the hot water in between the jars rather than immediately on top of them.

- Be sure that there is between one and two inches of hot water covering the tops of the jars that are immersed. In order to reach this level, you will need to add more water from the teakettle or saucepan that you have in reserve.

- Cover the kettle and bring the water to a full boil over high heat. Once the water has reached a full boil, reduce the heat to a medium boil and continue cooking for the period of time specified in the recipe.

- After the water has come to a boil, you should begin the processing time. Keep a boil going for the whole of the processing time.

- You will need to make adjustments to your processing time if you reside at an altitude that is higher than 1,000 feet above sea level.

The fifth step involves removing the jars that have been filled and checking their seals.

Do not attempt to adjust the bands or check the seals on the jars after the processing time has expired; instead, remove the jars from the boiling water using a jar lifter and set them on clean, dry kitchen towels or paper towels that are out of the way of drafts. Leave between one and two inches of space between each jar. The waiting time for the cooling might be anywhere from 12 to 24 hours. Do not under any circumstances attempt to speed up this procedure by chilling the jars. This might lead to the jars not sealing properly or the glass breaking.

After the jars have been allowed to fully cool, you should check the seals by pressing on the middle of the lid. A satisfactory vacuum seal may be determined if the lid has a solid feel and does not indent when pressed. When you apply pressure to the jar, if the lid depresses in the middle and produces a popping noise, it means that the jar is not sealed.

Unsealed jars should be refrigerated as soon as possible, and their contents should be used within two weeks or as directed by the recipe.

Reusing jars that have not been sealed.

There are a number of reasons why jars may not seal properly, including the following: you may have incorrectly estimated the processing time; food particles may not have been removed from the rim of the jar; you may have left an insufficient amount of headspace; or the sealant on the lids may have been faulty. When dealing with processed jars that did not seal properly, the safest and most convenient option is to immediately place the jar in the refrigerator and utilize the product within two weeks.

It is possible to reprocess jars that did not properly seal the first time around. However, bear in mind that the time it takes to reprocess your food is almost same to the amount of time it takes to make the meal from scratch. If none of the jars in the kettle seal, it is the sole circumstance in which it is necessary to reprocess the jars.

Follow these procedures to reprocess jars that have not been sealed:

- Take off the cover, and then throw it away.
- Examine the rim of the jar to see whether it has been damaged.
- If the jar is shattered, you should throw away the food within just in case a shard of glass made its way into the contents of the jar.
- Discard any damaged jars.

- Warm up the meal again.

You will find detailed instructions on how to fill your jars, how to remove any trapped air bubbles, and how to process your jars after they have been sterilized and filled.

- Repeat the processing of the filled jars for the amount of time specified in the recipe.
- After the jars have fully cooled, check the integrity of the seal.

The sixth step is to properly store your canned goods.

It is time to put away your canned goods after you have checked the seal and determined that it is intact (go to the section that came before this one for further information). To do this, please proceed as follows:

Take off the screw bands that are on your jars that are sealed.

Warm soapy water should be used to clean the screw bands and the jars that have been previously sealed.

This eliminates any residue that may have been left on the screw bands and jars.

Label each of your filled jars, being sure to include the processing date.

Keep your jars in a location that is cold, dark, and dry but do not use the screw bands.

How to Adjust Your Processing Times while Working at High Altitudes

If you are canning at an altitude that is more than 1,000 feet above sea level, you will need to change the amount of time that you process the food for safety reasons. At higher elevations, where there is less air, the temperature at which water boils is lower than

212 degrees. As a direct consequence of this, you will need to subject your food to a more extensive cooking procedure in order to eliminate any bacteria that have the potential to render your food poisonous.

If you reside at an altitude more than 1,000 feet above sea level, you should adhere to the following guidelines:

When dealing with durations of processing that are shorter than 20 minutes, you should add one extra minute for every additional 1,000 feet in altitude.

When dealing with durations of processing that are more than 20 minutes, add two extra minutes for every 1,000 feet of altitude.

I am grateful that you are using this book. I am sincerely concerned about the quality of your experience as a customer, and I am curious about how you have evaluated the process of reading this book. Your input, whether in the form of thoughts or opinions, is very much appreciated. I would appreciate it if you could let me know whether or not you were satisfied with the experience and whether or not you have any queries that you'd like answered. Thank you.

Chapter Four Safe Canning and Preserving

One thing that individuals who have been canning for a long time and others who have never canned before have in common is the desire and commitment to create a product that is tasty, safe to consume, and free from the danger of food illness. As long as you follow the correct methods and procedures for preparing, processing, and storing your food, the modern canning and preserving techniques that are employed today will give you with the results that you are looking for.

Take some time to go through this chapter before you start canning and preserving food. It will familiarize you with the microbes, enzymes, and other potentially harmful factors that lead to the rotting of food. You may also get information on how to spot spoiled food and how to prevent it from happening. Canning isn't something you should let the technical information in this chapter scare you away from doing. After reading this material, you won't need to worry about the safety of preparing and serving food that you've canned or preserved at home since you'll know exactly what to do.

Your Worries About Home-Preserved and Home-Canned Foods Will Be Put to Rest

Canning safely relies on avoiding deterioration of the product being preserved. Canning food at home has significantly improved and gotten safer over the years. Even though scientists have developed standardized processing processes, amateur canners have a better understanding of how to use these methods. If you canning and preserving foods at home by according to the most recent rules to the letter, you won't need to be too concerned about the products' level of freshness and safety.

In the sections that follow, you will find some advice on how to properly handle, prepare, and process your food.

Getting your meal ready in the right way.

Make sure the food you use is fresh and not beyond its prime. Be sure to give your food a thorough washing and thorough preparation to eliminate any dirt and bacteria: It should first be washed in a big bowl that has water and a few drops of detergent, and then it should be rinsed in a bowl that contains clean water. Preserve fruits and vegetables in jars as soon after picking them as you possibly can. No, you are not need to wash each individual berry: Place them in a colander, then immerse the whole colander, berries and all, in the wash dish. After that, give them a quick rinse under a stream of running water to remove any debris.

Take special care while packing your jars.

The manner in which the canning jars are filled is also a significant consideration:

- Avoid overpacking food items. If you try to jam an excessive amount of food into a jar, the food could not be properly processed since the heat won't be able to equally permeate it.

- Check that your jars have the appropriate amount of headspace. The term "headspace" refers to the volume of void space that exists between the underside of the lid and the highest point of the contents of the jar or container. Because of the expansion that happens when your jars are treated or when your food freezes, having enough headspace in them is essential to ensure the safety of the food you have preserved.

- Before placing the lid on the jar, you need to make sure that any air bubbles within have been removed. There will always be some air pockets within your jars, regardless of how neatly you pack them and fill them with contents.

- If you don't leave enough room at the top of your canning jars for the food to expand while it boils, the food you've preserved won't turn out as well. If there is not enough room in the jar for the expanding food, some of it may be forced out of the jar and under the lid, leaving food particles in the gap between the seal and the lip of the jar. If anything like this happens, the jar won't be able to form a vacuum seal.

- Leaving an excessive amount of room might cause the top layer of your meal to get discolored. If the processing time isn't long enough to exhaust the surplus air in the jar, your jar may have excessive headspace, which prevents it from generating a vacuum seal.

- Always be sure to utilize the headspace that is specified in the recipe. If the amount of headspace that is permitted is not specified in the recipe, use these guidelines:

- Leave a headspace of a quarter of an inch for liquids such as juice, jam, jelly, pickles, relish, chutney, and sauces & condiments.

- Leave a headspace of half an inch for items that are strong in acid, such as tomatoes and fruits.

- Leave a headspace of one inch for storing items that are low in acid, such as vegetables, meats, fish, and poultry.

Due to the fact that food expands as it freezes, leaving some headspace in the container in which you store it is essential when freezing food. If you do not allow the appropriate amount of headspace in your freezer container, the lid of the container might be pushed off, and the container itself could fracture or shatter. If your frozen food is allowed to come into direct contact with the air in your freezer, the quality of your food will suffer, and the food will develop a condition known as freezer burn. On the other side, having an excessive amount of air gap enables more air to enter your container. In spite of the fact that the food on the freezer does not have direct contact with the air, ice crystals may form in the top of the container where there is extra space. The quality of your food will decrease when it thaws due to the increased amount of fluids. If you don't trust your ability to estimate the headspace using your eyes alone, you may use a little plastic ruler that is about 6 inches long to accurately measure the headspace in the jar.

Getting all of the air bubbles out of your jars.

When you are filling your jars, the most essential thing to do is to pop any air bubbles that have been caught between the different bits of food. Although this may not appear significant at first glance, air bubbles may wreak havoc on the final product:

Jar stopper.

During processing, an excessive amount of pressure might develop within the jar as a result of the presence of air that has been trapped in air bubbles. During the time that the jar is being cooled, the pressure within the jar is higher than the pressure outside the jar. The process of sealing is hampered as a result of this imbalance.

Liquid levels.

Space is occupied by the air bubbles. When you cook food that has air that has been trapped between the different components of the meal before the jars are sealed, the amount of liquid in the jar will decrease. When you pack your food without the appropriate quantity of liquid in the jars, you run the risk of the food becoming discolored and floating during storage. The absence of air in tightly packed food makes room for sufficient liquid to fully cover the food while yet allowing for enough headroom.

Under no circumstances should you omit the procedure of expelling the air bubbles.

Selecting the appropriate canning process, and then completing all of the necessary steps.

- Always process your food in the appropriate manner for the food you are using. Can in a water bath any and all foods that are pickled or have a high acid content. Can under pressure all of the foods that have a low acid content. Proceed to the next section to learn how to figure out if a certain dish has a low, medium, or high amount of acidity. To prevent food from going bad, in addition to selecting the appropriate canning process, you need also take the following precautions:

- Don't try anything new and avoid taking any quick cuts. Make use of just tried and true procedures.

- Under no circumstances should you use an old recipe. Try to find a more recent version. Do not attempt to revise the instructions on your own. Make sure the date of publication is correct by looking at the beginning of the recipe book. If it is older than five years, you should look for a more recent version.

- If your location is at a height that is more than 1,000 feet above sea level, ensure that the processing time and pressure are adjusted appropriately for your altitude. For details on how altitude affects processing times, please refer to the section on "Adjusting your altitude"

- Do not remove the cover of the pressure canner in an effort to speed up the process of depressurizing the canner to zero pounds of pressure if you are pressure canning. Instead, wait for the canner to depressurize on its own.

- Your processed jars should be allowed to cool at room temperature without being disturbed.

• Make sure that your jars are processed for the appropriate length of time and, if you are using a pressure canner, at the appropriate pressure (both will be stated in your recipe). If you are at an altitude that is more than 1,000 feet above sea level, you will need to make modifications to the processing time and pressure.

• Before you put your food away, you should check the seal on each jar and take off the screw band.

Performing a check on your apparatus.

• To avoid waste, ensure that all of your equipment is in excellent condition and is operating as it should:

• It is important to check the accuracy of the pressure gauge and seal on your pressure canner on a yearly basis. (Testing is not required for gauges that use weights.) This may often be obtained at no cost from the extension office in your area.

• Jars and two-piece caps specifically designed for home canning should be used. Throw away any jars that have chips, cracks, or other damage.

• Sealing lids should never be used more than once. Always be sure you use fresh lids. The adhesive that forms the seal on the bottom of the lid can only be used after the container has been processed. If the lid of one of your jars does not seal properly after the first try, you should always use a new one. Despite the fact that we started with a brand new lid, there may be an issue with the sealant.

Understanding the Acidity Level of the Food You Eat

It is crucial to have a good understanding of the acidity level of the food you are processing since the pH, which is a measurement of acidity, will tell you whether you should can the food in a water bath or under pressure. For the purposes of preserving food by canning, food is classified into one of two groups according on the amount of acid it registers:

Fruits and foods that have been pickled are examples of foods that are high in acid. The pH of the foods included in this category is 4.6 or lower. Harmful bacteria are killed when they are processed in a canner that uses a water bath.

Tomatoes are categorized as a food that is low in sugar but rich in acid. Because there are so many different types of tomatoes available, it is now suggested that home canners add an acid to the process of canning in order to guarantee that the tomatoes will always have the appropriate level of acidity.

Foods that are low in acid, such as vegetables, meat, chicken, and fish, often have a low level of naturally occurring acid. The pH of these substances is more than 4.6. Put these goods through the canning process in a pressure cooker. This kind of cooker generates very high temperatures, which kills even the most heat-resistant microorganisms, such as botulism.

You may purchase litmus paper from places that sell educational supplies or scientific supplies, and then test the acidity level of your food on your own if you want to have the experience of being back in school for science all over again. Litmus paper is a kind of acid-sensitive paper that can determine the amount of acid present in food. It is also known as pH paper. The strip of pH paper that you put into your prepared meal causes the paper to change color as you do so. After that, you take the wet strip and compare it to the pH color chart that is included with the litmus paper.

The level of acidity or alkalinity in a meal is denoted by its pH, which stands for the potential of hydrogen. There is a range of values from

1 to 14. 7 is considered to be neutral. The lower the number, the more acidic the substance, and the higher the value, the more alkaline the substance. The pH value of your meal determines how acidic it is, and the lower it is, the more acidic it is.

Avoiding Spoilage.

The unwelcome and unneeded degeneration in canned or preserved food that renders it unsuitable for consumption is referred to as food spoiling. Consuming bad food may lead to a broad variety of illnesses, the specific symptoms of which are determined by the nature of the deterioration and the quantity of the food that is eaten. The symptoms may range from minor aches and pains, similar to those caused by the flu, to more severe diseases or even death.

However, despite the fact that there is a risk of the food being spoilt, you shouldn't let this deter you from canning. When you have a better understanding of how these tiny organisms and enzymes function, you will have a better understanding of why it is necessary to use the appropriate processing technique for the appropriate period of time in order to eliminate these potentially harmful food spoilers. And there is absolutely no need for concern on your part.

Confrontation with the spoilers

The four pathogens that may ruin food are mold, yeast, bacteria, and enzymes. Mold, yeast, and bacteria are all examples of microorganisms, which are distinct creatures despite their minuscule size.

Proteins found in both plants and animals may be classified as enzymes. When any one or more of the spoilers find themselves in an environment that is favorable for their growth, they expand extremely quickly and divide or reproduce every ten to thirty minutes! The rapid pace of this process makes it very clear how rapidly food may get spoiled. Some of them, like botulism, cause deterioration that is invisible to the human eye, while others, like mold, make their presence known in an obvious way.

There are living microorganisms in every environment, including your house, the dirt outside, and even the air that you breathe. It is often necessary to introduce microbes to foods in order to produce fermented goods such as bread or beer (for leavening).

They are also necessary for the production of antibiotics. What's the point? Microorganisms may be divided into two categories: those that cause sickness and those that cause food to deteriorate.

Mold.

Fungi with dried spores are what we refer to as mold. Jars containing high-acid foods or pickled foods that are not properly sealed provide these spores with the ideal conditions necessary to establish a colony. Once the spores have traveled through the air and landed on one of their preferred diets, the fungus will begin to germinate and develop. First, what seems to be silky strands, then color streaks, and lastly fuzz that covers the meal are what you observe when you look at the sample. Mold spores may be eliminated from food by using a water-bath canner to process high-acid and pickled foods.

Do not consume any food that has had the fuzz removed from it. At one point in time, this was considered risk-free; however, that is no longer the case. Mold releases carcinogens, some of which may be found in the food after it has been discarded. Consuming this food could make you sick, despite the fact that it seems to be clean and free of any pathogens.

Yeast.

Mold spores and yeast spores both develop on food in the same way. They have a particular fondness for foods that are strong in acidity and include a lot of sugar, such as jam or jelly. They seem as a thin layer of dry film that develops on the surface of your meal. By sterilizing your food in a water bath canner, you can eliminate the risk of yeast spores causing the food to become sour.

Bacteria.

Bacteria are a wide category of microorganisms that only have a single cell. Salmonella and staphylococcus are two examples of common bacteria. The most lethal sort of bacteria is botulism, which is also the one that should cause the greatest worry when canning since it may cause death. Because it has no odor and no visible color, it is very difficult to detect.

The spores that cause botulism are notoriously difficult to eradicate.

Spores of botulism despise meals that are rich in acid and pickled, but they are particularly fond of foods that are low in acid. When you place these spores in an environment that is devoid of oxygen and contains food that is low in acid, such as a jar of green beans, the spores will develop a poison in the food that will cause death to anybody who consumes it. Canning under pressure is the only method that can kill them in foods with a low acid content.

Before consuming any low-acid food that has been home-canned, ensure that it has been boiled for at least 15 minutes after it has reached a rolling boil at an elevation of 1,000 feet or less. When traveling at elevations higher than 1,000 feet, add one minute to your total travel time for every additional 1,000 feet in elevation.

The botany bacteria are not eliminated by boiling the water. Within 12 to 36 hours of consuming food contaminated with botulinum, symptoms of the disease will manifest themselves.

Those affected may have symptoms such as double vision as well as trouble eating, breathing, and speaking. If you feel that you may have consumed food that was contaminated, you should seek medical assistance as soon as possible. Antitoxins may be used to treat this poisoning; however, the sooner treatment can begin, the better.

Enzymes.

Proteins that are found naturally in plants and animals are referred to as enzymes. They promote the development and ripening of food, which has an effect on the taste, color, and texture of the food as well as the nutritional content. Temperatures between 85 to 120 degrees Fahrenheit are optimal for the activity of enzymes, as compared to temperatures below this range. They are not hazardous, but they may cause your food to become overripe and unappealing, in addition to creating an environment that is favorable for the growth of other microbes or bacteria.

When you slice or peel an apple, for instance, you are putting enzymes to work for you. After a short period of time, the apple will begin to turn brown. Applying an antioxidant solution to the apple after it has been chopped can stop the browning process. Blanching and hot packaging are two other procedures that may be used to stop the enzymatic activity in your food.

Adjusting your altitude.

Microorganisms may be killed when home-canned foods are subjected to the appropriate preparation. It is essential to be aware of your altitude since the temperature at which water boils and the pressure within a pressure canner both fluctuate at elevations of more than 1,000 feet above sea level. This is due to the fact that the air being breathed in at greater altitudes is less dense. When there is less resistance from the air, the temperature at which water boils is lower than 212 degrees.

Adjusting the processing time and pressure to account for the greater altitude can allow you to make food that is free of germs even when you are at higher altitudes. Because of these modifications, the temperature of your meal will be brought up to where it needs to be in order to kill any bacteria present.

If you are unsure about the elevation of the city in which you live, you may get this information by contacting the municipal offices, the public library, or the state or county cooperative extension agency that is listed in your local telephone directory. Simply type in the name of your city and state into the box located at the bottom of the page, click the "Submit" button, and then scroll down to see your city's elevation.

Identifying Foods That Have Become Putrid.

If you follow the specific instructions provided for each method of food preservation, you can rest assured that the likelihood of your home-canned foods going bad is significantly decreased. However, no one can guarantee that your home-canned foods will never go bad, even if they are stored properly. Do not taste your food if you have any cause to believe that it has gone bad or isn't functioning properly in any way. In addition, the fact that your food does not seem to be rotten does not guarantee that it is not.

- Visual inspection of your jars is the most effective method for determining whether or not food has gone bad. Examine the following items on the check list. If you are able to provide a "true" response to each of the following claims, the food that you have prepared should be OK to consume:

- The food in the jar has been completely submerged in liquid, packed to capacity, and the appropriate headspace has been preserved.

- The food in the jar does not have any air bubbles that are moving about in it.

- The jars feature seals that are strong and secure.

- The hue of the meal has remained consistent throughout.

- The meal is neither crumbly or mushy in any way.

- The liquid contained in the jar is transparent, devoid of any cloudiness, and clean of any sediment.

- When you are certain that your food has satisfied the requirements of the prior checklist, go to a more thorough inspection of the jars. If you find any signs of spoiling at any point throughout this procedure, you should not continue your search but rather dispose of your goods in the appropriate manner.

- Keep the jar at around chest height.

- Check the underside of the lid of the jar for any seepage or seeping that would suggest a damaged seal. Turn and rotate the jar while you check.

- Check the top of the food to see if there are any dried food specks or streaks that started at the top of the jar.

- Examine the contents to see if there are any air bubbles that are rising and any colors that are not natural. The cloudiness should not be present in either the meal or the beverage.

- Open the jar.

- There shouldn't be any liquid oozing out of the hole.

- Examine the odor of what's within the jar.

- Note whether there are any scents that are not natural or that are strange.

- Examine the top of your food surface as well as the bottom of the lid for any growth that looks like cotton and is often white, blue, black, or green.

It's possible that spoiled low-acid food will show little to no visible signs that it's gone bad. Assume that any jars that are under suspicion contain botulinum toxins and treat them accordingly. Never use or eat any canned food that shows indications of deterioration or that you fear may already be rotten. This includes both using and tasting the food.

If you remove the screw bands from the jars after they have been cooled and sealed, you will be able to readily notice any broken seals or food that is pouring out from beneath the lid, which are both signs that the food has gone bad.

Chapter Five Fruits and Veggies Recipe

Chutney made with apples

Time Required for Preparation: 10 Minutes

Serving size is eight jars of 11 ounces each.

- Ingredients:
- 2 cups of unfiltered white vinegar 2 teaspoons salt
- 2 teaspoons of cinnamon that has been ground 2 teaspoons of ginger in powdered form
- 2 measuring cups of white sugar 2 measuring cups of dark sugar 1 pound. raisins
- 2 jalapeño peppers, chopped 1 cup of chopped onions 1 cup of chopped apples (10 medium), cored and diced

Directions:

- Put the ingredients into a saucepan with a thick bottom and cook them until the mixture is thick, which should take approximately an hour.
- Pour the mixture into jars that have been previously sterilized, being sure to leave approximately half an inch of headspace. Jars may be processed by immersing them in a water bath for twenty minutes.
- Take the jars out of the oven and set them down on a dish towel to cool.

- Relish the taste whenever you need it with the delicacy of your choice.

Calorie content: 43 kilocalories

Blueberries that have been canned.

Time Required for Preparation: 20 Minutes

Serving size is six jars of 11 ounces each.

Ingredients:

- 8 cups blueberries
- 2 cups sugar

Directions:

- Put the blueberries in a saucepan with a heavy bottom, cover them with sugar, and stir to combine. Hold in place for one hour.

- Adjust the heat to medium and continue to simmer for another 10 minutes, or until the blueberries release their juices. When this occurs, remove the pot from the heat and immediately transfer the berries to hot jars that have been previously steriled.

- Clean the rims of the jars, then screw the lids on tightly. Twenty minutes should be spent with the object completely submerged in a bath of hot water.

- Take the jars out of the oven and let them to cool on a tea towel.

- Relish the taste whenever you need it with the delicacy of your choice.

215 calories (kcal) in total.

Cherries preserved in a can.

Time Required for Preparation: 10 Minutes

There are 8 servings per 11-ounce jar.

Ingredients:

- a single quart of water 3 cups sugar
- 5 kg of cherries, cored

Directions:

- To dissolve the sugar in the boiling water, you may use a saucepan.
- After this, put the cherries in the pan and stir them around. Pour the mixture into jars that have been cleaned, being sure to leave a space of half an inch at the top of each jar.
- Jars' rims should be cleaned and then secured.
- Jars should be completely submerged in a water bath containing boiling water for a period of 15 minutes. Take the jars out of the oven and set them down on a dish towel to cool.
- If you wish to preserve cherry pie filling, you must first bring the cherries to a boil and then reduce the heat to a simmer for ten minutes before transferring the filling to jam jars.
- Relish the taste whenever you need it with the delicacy of your choice.

The food has 149 calories.

Grapes

Time Required for Preparation: 20 Minutes

Servings: 1-quart jar.

Ingredients:

- One pound of red grapes
- 14 tsp of ground cloves
- ½ vanilla bean
- a single stick of cinnamon
- 1 cup sugar
- 1/4 mug of water
- 1 cup apple cider vinegar
- 14 of a teaspoon of ground black pepper 1/8 of a teaspoon of mustard seed, yellow

Directions:

- First, remove the stems from the grapes and wash them well. First, cut off the end that was connected to the stem, and then put it to the side.

- Put the sugar, water, and vinegar into a pot and bring them to a boil over high heat. Put all of the spices into the bottom of a jar with a capacity of 1 quart. The grapes should be placed into the container.

- After you have poured the brine over the grapes, cover the jar with the lid.

- After the used jar has had time to cool, put it in the refrigerator so that it may sit for a full day.

- Relish the taste whenever you need it with the delicacy of your choice.

152 calories (kcal) in total.

Prunes.

Time Required for Preparation: 15 Minutes

Servings: 1-quart jar.

Ingredients:

- 1 bay leaf 1-star anise
- two berries of allspice
- 2 green cardamom pods
- 1/8 teaspoon red chili flakes
- a quarter of a teaspoon of cloves and a quarter of a teaspoon of black peppercorns 1 grain of ginger, grated, 1 fourth of a cup of honey
- 1/4 cup of dark brown sugar
- 1 blood orange, with the peel removed but the fruit intact 1 cup of red wine vinegar for 1 pound of meat Prunes pitted A little bit of salt

Directions:

- To get started, combine the prunes and the red wine vinegar in a pot of medium size. Mix the ingredients together, then add in the zest of the blood orange as well as the juice from the blood orange.
- Simmer for 20 minutes. Take the pan off the heat.

- After the prunes have cooled to room temperature, place them in the jar.

- Remove the lid, give it a good cleaning, and replace it. After it has reached room temperature and remained there for some time, put the jar in the refrigerator.

- Relish the taste whenever you need it with the delicacy of your choice.

Calorie content: 246 kilocalories

Cranberries.

Time Required for Preparation: 30 Minutes

Serving size is four jars of 11 ounces each.

Ingredients:

- Cranberries to the tune of 24 ounces
- 1 tablespoon of ground allspice
- 2 sticks of cinnamon in total
- 2 cups sugar
- 3 cups apple cider vinegar
- ¼ teaspoon juniper berries
- 1/2 milligram of ground black pepper
- cloves, one-half of a teaspoon

Directions:

- To begin, wash the cranberries and remove any cranberries or stems that are damaged or imperfect. Sugar and vinegar should be combined in a pot before being brought up to a boil using medium heat. Put the cinnamon sticks in the dish.

- Put the cloves, allspice, and peppercorns in a spice bag. Also include the juniper berries. Put the bag in the saltwater solution. When the brine has reached a boil, add the cranberries and give them a good stir.

- Wait seven minutes before checking the progress.

- After the mixture has finished cooking, take it off the fire and remove the spice bag as well as the cinnamon sticks. Both cinnamon sticks should be snapped in half lengthwise, and then placed aside.

- Take the cranberries out of the brine with a spoon and put them in the jars once you've dried them off. Cranberries will benefit from having brine poured over them.

- Keep a gap of approximately half an inch at the very top of the jars. Put one-half of a cinnamon stick in each of the jars. After the lids have been cleaned, place them back on the jars.

- Jars should be completely submerged in a water bath containing boiling water for ten minutes.

- After this, take the jars out of the oven and set them down on a tea towel so that they may cool down. After they have cooled down enough to handle, put them in the refrigerator. Allow them to sit for a full day.

- Relish the taste whenever you need it with the delicacy of your choice.

Calorie content: 158 kilocalories

Pickles made from watermelon.

Time Required for Preparation: 30 Minutes

Servings: four to five jars of 11 ounces each.

Ingredients:

- two tablespoons of ground cloves
- cinnamon sticks measuring 15 inches, chopped up into pieces 1 and 12 cups of water
- 1 and 12 cups of regular vinegar 6 liters of water
- 1 watermelon weighing ten pounds 1/3 cup pickling salt
- 3 ½ cup sugar

Directions:

- First cut away the watermelon's skin, and then cut away the lighter areas on the outside. Discard.
- You should have around 9 cups of watermelon after cutting it into pieces that are 1 inch in size. Put the pieces of watermelon into a big mixing bowl that is not made of metal.
- Combine the pickling salt with six cups of water. Pour this mixture over the watermelon, and let it sit like this overnight. Rinse the watermelon well with cold water after placing it in a strainer. Put the watermelon in a saucepan with a capacity of 4 quarts and cover it with ice water.
- Bring the mixture to a boil. Turn the heat down to low and simmer for twenty-five minutes.
- Put one and a half cups of water, vinegar, cloves, cinnamon sticks, and sugar in a saucepan and bring to

a boil. Turn the heat down and continue to cook for another 10 minutes. After straining, set aside the liquid.

- Bring the syrup to a boil, then stir in the watermelon. Cover the pot and bring the heat down to a simmer for the next half an hour.

- Put the watermelon and the syrup in the jars, but be sure to leave about half an inch of headspace at the top of each jar.

- Jars should be completely submerged in the water bath for ten minutes. Take the jars out of the oven and set them down on a clean dish towel to cool.

- Relish the taste whenever you need it with the delicacy of your choice.

Calorie content: 70 kilocalories

Blueberry Pie Filling.

Time Required for Preparation: 15 Minutes

Serving size is six jars of 11 ounces each.

Ingredients:

- a total of six cups of fresh blueberries

- ½ cup lemon juice 7 gallons of ice-cold water 6 cups sugar

Directions:

- Blueberries should be washed and then drained.

- Put the blueberries and enough water into a big saucepan, cover them, and bring them to a boil for five minutes. Drain the water after this.

- Bring the sugar, lemon juice, water, and fruit pectin to a boil in a big saucepan. Combine these ingredients. After the blueberries have been well combined, remove the pan from the heat.

- After the jars have been sterilized, pour the contents inside, being sure to leave a half an inch of headspace.

- After the rims have been cleaned, fasten them to the jars. Place the jars in a bath of boiling water and let them to remain there for twenty-five minutes.

- Take the jars out of the oven and set them on the counter to cool.

- Relish the taste whenever you need it with the delicacy of your choice.

Calorie content: 474 kilocalories

Apple Pie Filling.

Time Required for Preparation: 15 Minutes

Serving size is four jars of 11 ounces each.

Ingredients:

- 5 cups lemon juice
- ¾ cup nutmeg (optional) 2 ½ cups apple juice
- 1 level teaspoon of ice-cold water 1 ½ cups cinnamon
- 5 ½ cups fruit pectin 6 cups sugar
- 7 crisp apples, peeled, cored, and thinly sliced.

Directions:

- Cook the apples for 5 minutes in a big saucepan using 6 cups of boiling water, after which they should be drained.

- Mix the fruit pectin, sugar, and cinnamon with the water and apple juice in a separate saucepan before adding it to the apple juice and water. Bring the liquid to a boil, and then sprinkle in the nutmeg.

- When the mixture has reached the point where it is beginning to thicken, add the lemon juice and continue to simmer for another minute. Pour the mixture into jars that have been previously sterilized, being sure to leave approximately half an inch of headspace.

- Jars' rims and lids should be cleaned before being screwed on. The jars should be left out on the counter to cool.

- Relish the taste whenever you need it with the delicacy of your choice.

74 calories per 100 grams.

Cinnamon Banana Butter.

Time Required for Preparation: 15 Minutes

Jars of 11 ounces each make up a serving.

Ingredients:

- a half of a teaspoon of cinnamon powder 3 teaspoons vanilla

- 4 ½ cups sugar packet fruit pectin 1/3 cup fresh lemon juice 4 cups of bananas mixed together.

Directions:

- Pectin may be dissolved by heating lemon juice, bananas, and pectin in a saucepan until the pectin is completely dissolved. Bring to a boil while continuously stirring the mixture. Mix the sugar into the mixture.

- After bringing the mixture to a full and rolling boil while stirring it continually, take it off the heat and stir in the vanilla and cinnamon.

- Pour the mixture into jars that have been previously sterilized, being sure to leave approximately half an inch of headspace. After cleaning the rims and lids, place them back on the jars. Jars should be completely submerged in a water bath containing boiling water for ten minutes.

- Take out the empty jars and place them on a clean dish towel on the counter where they can cool.

- Relish the taste whenever you need it with the delicacy of your choice.

73 calories (kcal) in total.

Carrots with a Spicy Kick

Time Required for Preparation: 20 Minutes

Servings: four to five jars of 11 ounces each.

Ingredients:

- 2 quarts fresh carrots
- 1 cup sugar
- 2 cups cider vinegar
- half a teaspoon's worth of celery seed
- ¼ piece mace

- 14 of a cinnamon stick
- cloves to the measure of a quarter teaspoon
- 1/4 teaspoon of ground allspice
- ¼ teaspoon salt

Directions:

- Put the salt and the spices in a little bag made of cotton and tie it closed. Bring the sugar, vinegar, and spices to a boil and let them simmer for 15 minutes.
- Prepare the jar for use by placing it in boiling water for about fifteen minutes. After removing the sterile jar from the water, the vinegar mixture should be added to the jar.
- After cleaning the rim and the lid, reattach it to the jar, and then put it somewhere out of the way for approximately two weeks. Take out the bag of spices. After cooking the fresh carrots until they are soft but still have some bite to them, set them aside to cool.
- While the vinegar is heating, add a half cup of the liquid from the carrots. After adding the carrots, continue to cook over a low heat for 15 minutes.
- Carrots should be packed into sterile jars, and the vinegar mixture should be poured over them. Mix it up to get rid of any air bubbles. Jars' rims and lids should be cleaned before being screwed on. Jars should be completely submerged in a water bath containing boiling water for ten minutes.
- Relish the taste whenever you need it with the delicacy of your choice.

Calorie content: 15 kilocalories

Pressure Mushrooms that are canned.

Time needed for preparation is between 15 and 20 minutes.

Servings: 18.

- Ingredients.
- 3 ½ tsp. salt.
- 7 pound. mushrooms.

Directions.

- A pot should be put over medium-high heat, and the water and mushrooms should be added to the pot. Bring it to a boil, then continue to simmer it for another 5 minutes.
- After you have drained the combination, do not get rid of the hot liquid; instead, put it to the side.
- Place the sliced mushrooms in the bottom of sterile jars, then pour the remaining cooking liquid over the mushrooms until the jars are full. It is important to remember to allow a gap of one inch at the top of the jar. After removing any air bubbles from the jars' interiors with a tiny knife and replacing their lids, place the jars in the refrigerator. Wipe the rims clean with a dish towel, then check to be that they are securely fastened;
- After pressurizing the jars for 45 minutes at a pressure of 10 pounds, take them from the canner and let them to cool on a wooden surface. After the jars have been pressurized, remove them from the canner and allow them to cool on a wooden surface. After they have cooled down, put them away in a location where it is dark.

- Relish the taste whenever you need it with the delicacy of your choice.

Calories: 89

Pressure Asparagus preserved in a can

Time needed for preparation is between 10 and 15 minutes.

Servings: 24 Ingredients.

- 6 pound. asparagus.

Directions.

- Asparagus that has been trimmed and sliced into pieces measuring 1 inch.
- Put them in a saucepan with water that is already boiling. They should be cooked for three minutes over medium-high heat once the pot has been placed on the stove.
- After draining the asparagus, do not get rid of the hot liquid; instead, put it to the side.
- After the asparagus has been placed in the bottom of the sterile jars, fill the jars with the cooking liquid that was saved. It is important to remember to allow a gap of one inch at the top of the jar. After removing any air bubbles from the jars' interiors with a tiny knife and replacing their lids, place the jars in the refrigerator. Use a kitchen towel to clean the rims, and check to be that the lids are securely fastened before proceeding.
- Place the jars into the pressure canner, and then subject them to a pressure of ten pounds for a period of thirty minutes.

- After the jars have been subjected to high pressure, take them from the pressure canner and allow them to cool on a surface made of wood. After they have cooled down, put them away in a location where it is dark.
- Relish the taste whenever you need it with the delicacy of your choice.

Calories: 70

Onions cured in salt water.

Time needed for preparation is between 15 and 20 minutes.

Servings: 8.

Ingredients.

- 1 pint Water.
- between 6 and 8 Onions (medium, peeled, and thinly sliced).
- 3 tbsp Canning salt.

Directions.

- Put the water and salt in a dish and stir them together.
- Place onions into the canning jars.
- After the jars have been filled with the brine, pack the onions tightly into the jars.
- After you have sealed the jars, store them in a cool location for three to four weeks while covering them with clean muslin cloth.
- Check the jars every day to ensure that the onions are covered with water, and after three to four weeks, store the jars in the refrigerator.

- Relish the taste whenever you need it with the delicacy of your choice.

Calories: 80.

Vegetable and beef.

Time required for preparation: 45–50 minutes

Servings: 12.

Ingredients.

- 12 cups of frozen peas in the cup.
- 12 fluid ounces of water.
- a pair of onions
- 6 pound. hamburgers.
- 11 individual cloves of garlic
- 3 g of pepper that has been minced.
- 10 cups of beef stock to be exact.
- 10 pound potatoes.
- 4 tsp salt.

Directions.

- To prepare the onions, peel them and then cube them.
- First, the garlic cloves need to be peeled and then minced.
- First, the potatoes need to be peeled and then sliced.
- Place the burger, the pepper, and the salt in a saucepan and bring it up to a temperature of medium-high. Cook it until the color changes to brown. The fat should then be drained and stored aside.

- Place the meat in the jars starting from the bottom. The next step is to put one teaspoon of minced garlic, potatoes, onions, and frozen peas into each individual container. You may guarantee that the jar can hold additional potatoes by pressing them down with your finger to make extra room. Remember to allow a gap of one quarter of an inch at the top of the jar.
- Add water and beef stock until it reaches the same level as the potatoes. After removing any air bubbles from the jars' interiors with a tiny knife and replacing their lids, place the jars in the refrigerator. Use a kitchen towel to clean the rims, and check to be that the lids are securely fastened before proceeding.
- Place the jars into the pressure canner and process them under pressure for ninety minutes while maintaining a pressure of ten pounds.
- After the jars have been subjected to pressure, take them from the canner and allow them to cool for five minutes on a surface made of wood. After they have cooled down, put them away in a location where it is dark.
- To prepare the onions, peel them and then cube them.
- The garlic cloves should be peeled and then minced, while the potatoes should be peeled and then sliced.
- Place the burger, the pepper, and the salt in a saucepan and bring it up to a temperature of medium-high. Cook it until the color changes to brown. The fat should then be drained and stored aside.
- Place the meat in the jars starting from the bottom. The next step is to put one teaspoon of minced garlic, potatoes, onions, and frozen peas into each

individual container. You may guarantee that the jar can hold additional potatoes by pressing them down with your finger to make extra room.

- Remember to allow a gap of one quarter of an inch at the top of the jar.
- Add water and beef stock until it reaches the same level as the potatoes. After removing any air bubbles from the jars' interiors with a tiny knife and replacing their lids, place the jars in the refrigerator. Use a kitchen towel to clean the rims, and check to be that the lids are securely fastened before proceeding.
- Place the jars into the pressure canner and process them under pressure for ninety minutes while maintaining a pressure of ten pounds.
- After the jars have been subjected to pressure, take them from the canner and allow them to cool for five minutes on a surface made of wood. After they have cooled down, put them away in a location where it is dark.
- Relish the taste whenever you need it with the delicacy of your choice.

Calories: 157

Cucumbers that live in saltwater.

Time needed for preparation is between 15 and 20 minutes.

Servings: 10.

Ingredients.

- ¼ cup Dill 20 individual garlic cloves (peeled).
- 2 quarts Water.
- 4 kg of cucumbers for pickling.

- 1/2 cup of salt for canning.

Directions.

- The blossoms of cucumbers should be washed and then clipped.
- In a saucepan that is heated at a medium temperature, combine the water and salt. Make water boil.
- At the very bottom of a jar, layer some garlic and cucumbers.
- Put some seawater in each of the jars.
- After you have sealed the jars, store them in a cool location for three to four weeks while covering them with clean muslin cloth.
- Make sure that the cucumbers are covered with water at all times and check the jars every day.
- After three or four weeks, the jars were transferred to the refrigerator.
- Relish the taste whenever you need it with the delicacy of your choice.

Calories: 72.

Beets packed under pressure and canned.

Time needed for preparation is between 10 and 15 minutes.

Servings: 12.

Ingredients.

- 6 pound. beets.

Directions.

- Be sure to trim the beets.
- Place the beets in a saucepan that is filled with water that is already boiling. They should be cooked for twenty-five minutes with the saucepan placed over medium-high heat.
- After draining the beets, do not get rid of the hot liquid; instead, put it to the side.
- Beets should first have their skins peeled off before being sliced.
- Place the beets in the bottom of the sterilized jars, then fill the jars with the cooking liquid that was prepared earlier. It is important to remember to allow a gap of one inch at the top of the jar. After removing any air bubbles from the jars' interiors with a tiny knife and replacing their lids, place the jars in the refrigerator. Use a kitchen towel to clean the rims, and check to be that the lids are securely fastened before proceeding.
- Place the jars into the pressure canner, and then subject them to a pressure of ten pounds for a period of thirty minutes.
- After the jars have been subjected to high pressure, take them from the pressure canner and allow them to cool on a surface made of wood. After they have cooled down, put them away in a location where it is dark.
- Relish the taste whenever you need it with the delicacy of your choice.

Calories: 68.

Chapter Six Preserves, Conserves, and Some Marmalades

Kumquats Marmalade

Time Required for Preparation: 5 Minutes

Servings: 2 (½ pint) jars.

Ingredients:

- ½ cup sugar
- 2 cups of chopped kumquats, plus 12 cup of water
- A little bit of ground cinnamon as well as ground cardamom

Directions:

- Place kumquats into a pot. First add some ground cinnamon, then some ground cardamom, some sugar, and some water, and then combine everything. Cover it and let it rest at room temperature for two to three hours to enable the fruit to macerate. For even more flavor, place it in the refrigerator overnight.

- Cook using a pot set over a heat source that is anywhere between medium and high, and then bring the mixture to a simmer while stirring it constantly. Turn the heat down to medium and continue cooking while stirring constantly for ten minutes.

- Take the pan off the heat. Allow between 5 and 10 minutes for it to cool.

- Spoon heated marmalade into sterilized jars. Wrap it up, and let it sit out until it reaches room temperature. Place in the refrigerator to cool.

- Relish the taste whenever you need it with the delicacy of your choice.

34.9 kilocalories of energy

Super Tangy Marmalade.

Time Required for Preparation: 5 Minutes

Servings: 3-4 (½ pint) jars.

Ingredients:

- 1 and a half cups of granulated white sugar

- 1 cup of limes, unpeeled and cut very thinly, but not peeled 1 cup of lemons, not peeled and cut very thinly. 3 liters of water

Direction:

- Combine the citrus slices and water in a heavy-bottomed saucepan or other kind of cooking pot. Bring the mixture to a boil, then reduce the heat and let it simmer for a few minutes.

- Sugar should be well incorporated.

- Bring the mixture to a boil and continue boiling until the thermometer reaches 220 degrees Fahrenheit. Continue boiling the mixture for another 25 to 30 minutes over medium heat until it becomes firm and thick. Continuously stir the pot

- When you are finished, use a jar funnel to transfer the hot mixture into the jars that have been previously sterilized. Keep a headspace that is a quarter of an inch from the top of the jar.

- Make use of a spatula made of a material other than metal and swirl the mixture gently in order to eliminate the minute air bubbles. After this, you should use a moist cloth to clean the margins of the seal. After that, screw the tops back onto the jars. Also, be sure to fix the bands or rings so that they close properly and there is no leaking.

- Put the jars somewhere dry and dark to store them. Please allow it to cool. Keep in the refrigerator, and consume within the next week.

- Relish the taste whenever you need it with the delicacy of your choice.

Calorie content: 41 kilocalories

Marmalade made with onions and garlic

Time Required for Preparation: 5 Minutes

Servings: 2-3 (1 pint) jars.

Ingredients:

- 4 to 5 cups of sweet onions, cut very thinly 1 tablespoon of vinegar made from red wine

- 1/2 teaspoon of dark brown sugar

- 1 tenth of a spoonful of butter

- a half teaspoon of salt and three chopped garlic cloves a quarter of a teaspoon of black pepper

Directions:

- Mix the sugar, onion, and garlic together in a large frying pot or a saucepan with a deep bottom. Bring the mixture to a boil, then continue to simmer it for another 25–30 minutes over medium heat. Maintain a constant stirring. Combine the butter, vinegar, salt, and pepper in a mixing bowl.

- Bring the mixture to a boil and continue cooking it for another 10–12 minutes over medium heat until it reaches the desired consistency of being firm and thick. Maintain a constant stirring.

- After that, use a jar funnel to transfer the heated mixture into the jars that have been previously sterilized. Always leave a headspace of a quarter of an inch from the top of the jar. Make use of a spatula made of a material other than metal and mix gently in order to eliminate minute air bubbles.

- When you're through, use a moist towel to clean the edges. Put the lids on the jars and tighten the bands or rings to ensure a good seal and avoid any leaks.

- Put the jars somewhere dry and dark to store them. Please allow it to cool.

- Refrigerate the marmalade and consume it within a week's time at the very most.

- Relish the taste whenever you need it with the delicacy of your choice.

121 calories (kcal) in total.

Ginger Orange Marmalade.

Time Required for Preparation: 20 Minutes

Servings: 2-3 (1/2 pint) jars.

- Ingredients:
- 6-7 bitter oranges 2 mugs' worth of water
- 1 medium lemon
- 3 cups granulated sugar
- 1 and 14 teaspoons of ginger that has been peeled and grated

Directions:

- Peel the oranges and lemons, then cut them into thin strips after removing the peels.
- Oranges and lemons should each be cut in half lengthwise. Extract the juice, take out the seeds, and put the juice aside; however, do not throw away the pulp.
- Combine the water, pulp, juice, and skins of the fruit in a cooking pot or a saucepan with a deep lid.
- Bring the mixture to a boil, then reduce it to a simmer for 45 to 50 minutes, or until the strips are tender. Incorporate the sugar and ginger into the mixture.
- Bring the mixture to a boil and continue cooking it over medium heat until it reaches the desired consistency of being firm and thick. Continuously stir the pot
- When you are finished, use a jar funnel to transfer the hot mixture into the jars that have been previously sterilized. Keep a headspace that is a quarter of an inch from the top of the jar.
- Make use of a spatula made of a material other than metal and swirl the mixture gently in order to eliminate the

minute air bubbles. After this, you should use a moist cloth to clean the margins of the seal. After that, put the lids on the jars. Also, be sure to fix the bands or rings so that they close properly and there is no leaking.

- Put the jars somewhere dry and dark to store them. Please allow it to cool. Keep in the refrigerator, and consume within a week of storage.

- Relish the taste whenever you need it with the delicacy of your choice.

73 calories (kcal) in total.

Tangy Tomato.

Time Required for Preparation: 15 Minutes

Servings: 3-4 (½ pint) jars.

Ingredients:

- 1 cup sugar

- 1/4 cup of honey

- 2 lemons, not peeled, but sliced and seeded, medium size 2 and a half pounds worth of yellow tomatoes

- 2 troy ounces of grated ginger

Directions:

- Combine the water and tomatoes in a large cooking pot or a saucepan with a deep bottom. Bring the mixture to a boil, then reduce the heat to a simmer to soften the tomatoes.

- Tomatoes should have the seeds removed before being chopped.

- Mix the diced tomatoes, honey, and sugar in a heavy-bottomed saucepan or other kind of cooking pot.

- Put it away for at least a few hours, or you may opt to leave it out all night. Mix in the ginger and lemon juice.

- Bring the mixture to a boil and continue cooking it over medium heat until it reaches the desired consistency of being firm and thick. Continuously stir the pot

- When you are finished, use a jar funnel to transfer the hot mixture into the jars that have been previously sterilized. Keep a headspace that is a quarter of an inch from the top of the jar.

- Make use of a spatula made of a material other than metal and swirl the mixture gently in order to eliminate the minute air bubbles. After this, you should use a moist cloth to clean the margins of the seal. After that, put the lids on the jars. Also, be sure to fix the bands or rings so that they close properly and there is no leaking.

- Put the jars somewhere dry and dark to store them. Please allow it to cool. Keep in the refrigerator, and consume within a week of storage.

- Relish the taste whenever you need it with the delicacy of your choice.

124 calories per 100 grams.

Preserve made from black currants.

Time Required for Preparation: 10 Minutes

Servings: 4 (½ pint) jars.

Ingredients:

- 4 and a half cups of crushed black currants

- ¼ cup lemon juice

- 3 cups granulated sugar 1 cup of water 1 tablespoon of zest from a lemon A little bit of salt

Directions:

- Put all of the ingredients into a pot or a large saucepan and mix them together.

- Bring the mixture to a boil and continue boiling it until the thermometer reaches 220 degrees Fahrenheit. Continue boiling the mixture for approximately 30 minutes over medium heat until it becomes firm and thick. Maintain a constant stirring.

- When you are finished, use a jar funnel to transfer the hot mixture into the jars that have been previously sterilized. Keep a headspace that is a quarter of an inch from the top of the jar.

- Make use of a spatula made of a material other than metal and swirl the mixture gently in order to eliminate the minute air bubbles. After this, you should use a moist cloth to clean the margins of the seal. After that, put the lids on the jars. Also, be sure to fix the bands or rings so that they close properly and there is no leaking.

- Put the jars somewhere dry and dark to store them. Please allow it to cool. Keep in the refrigerator, and consume within a week of storage.

- Relish the taste whenever you need it with the delicacy of your choice.

Calorie content: 52 kilocalories

Preserves made using watermelon and lemon.

Time Required for Preparation: 15 Minutes

Servings: 4 (½ pint) jars.

Ingredients:

- watermelon, peeled, seeded, and cubed (weight in pounds)
- watermelon 3 cups of granulated white sugar lemons that have not been peeled, cut, or seeded

Instructions:

- Place the watermelon cubes, lemon slices, and sugar in a heavy-bottomed cooking pot or a large saucepan. Mix well.

- Bring the mixture to a boil, then continue to simmer it for approximately two hours over a medium heat until it is frothy and thick. Maintain a constant stirring.

- When you are finished, use a jar funnel to transfer the hot mixture into the jars that have been previously sterilized. Keep a headspace that is a quarter of an inch from the top of the jar.

- Make use of a spatula made of a material other than metal and swirl the mixture gently in order to eliminate the minute air bubbles. After this, you should use a moist cloth to clean the margins of the seal. After that, put the lids on the jars. Also, be sure to fix the bands or rings so that they close properly and there is no leaking.

- Put the jars somewhere dry and dark to store them. Please allow it to cool. Place in the coldest part of your refrigerator.

- Relish the taste whenever you need it with the delicacy of your choice.

Number of calories: 224

Preserved Apples with Lemon

Time Required for Preparation: 5 Minutes

Servings: 3-4 (½ pint) jars.

Ingredients:

- 3 cups of apples that have been cored, peeled, and sliced.
- a half cup of water and a teaspoon of nutmeg powder
- ½ tbsp lemon juice
- 1 lemon, cut, seeded, and unpeeled to begin with
- 1 packet of powdered pectin (equal to 0.75 ounces) 2 cups sugar

Directions:

- Combine the apples, water, sugar, lemon juice, and lemon slices in a heavy-bottomed saucepan or other kind of cooking pot.
- Bring the mixture to a boil, then continue to simmer it for another 8 to 10 minutes over medium heat until it becomes firm and thick. Maintain a constant stirring.
- Pectin and nutmeg should be mixed in together.

- Bring the mixture to a boil and continue cooking it over medium heat until it reaches the desired consistency of being firm and thick. Maintain a constant stirring.

- When you are finished, use a jar funnel to transfer the hot mixture into the jars that have been previously sterilized. Keep a headspace that is a quarter of an inch from the top of the jar.

- Make use of a spatula made of a material other than metal and swirl the mixture gently in order to eliminate the minute air bubbles. After this, you should use a moist cloth to clean the margins of the seal. After that, put the lids on the jars. Also, be sure to fix the bands or rings so that they close properly and there is no leaking.

- Used jars should be sterilized in a water bath for about ten minutes. Put the jars somewhere dry and dark to store them. Please allow it to cool. Store in your refrigerator

- Relish the taste whenever you need it with the delicacy of your choice.

Calorie content: 50 kilocalories

Preserve made with lemon and peaches.

Time Required for Preparation: 15 Minutes

Servings: 4 (½ pint) jars.

Ingredients:

- Two huge lemons' worth of juice One pound of peaches, peeled, pitted, and chopped 1 ½ cups granulated sugar

Directions:

- Mix the peaches, lemon juice, and sugar together in a large cooking pot or a saucepan with a deep bottom.

- Put the mixture in the fridge for two to four hours.

- Bring the mixture to a boil and continue boiling it until the thermometer reaches 220 degrees Fahrenheit. Continue cooking the mixture for approximately one to two hours over medium heat until it is firm and thick. Continuously stir the pot

- When you are finished, use a jar funnel to transfer the hot mixture into the jars that have been previously sterilized. Keep a headspace that is a quarter of an inch from the top of the jar.

- Make use of a spatula made of a material other than metal and swirl the mixture gently in order to eliminate the minute air bubbles. After this, you should use a moist cloth to clean the margins of the seal. After that, put the lids on the jars. Also, be sure to fix the bands or rings so that they close properly and there is no leaking.

- Used jars should be sterilized in a water bath for about ten minutes. Put the jars somewhere dry and dark to store them. Please allow it to cool. Place in the coldest part of your refrigerator.

- Relish the taste whenever you need it with the delicacy of your choice.

Calorie content: 50 kilocalories

Preserve made from pears and ginger.

Time Required for Preparation: 10 Minutes

Servings: 3-4 (1/2 pint) jars.

Ingredients:

- 2 cups pears. cut, peeled, and seeded chunks
- ½ teaspoon salt 2 and a half cups honey
- 1 lemon, peeled and cut into small pieces

Instructions:

- Combine all of the ingredients in a large cooking pot or a saucepan with a high sides.

- Bring the mixture to a boil and continue cooking it for another 12–15 minutes over medium heat until it reaches the desired consistency of being firm and thick. Continuously stir the pot

- When you are finished, use a jar funnel to transfer the hot mixture into the jars that have been previously sterilized. Keep a headspace that is a quarter of an inch from the top of the jar.

- Make use of a spatula made of a material other than metal and swirl the mixture gently in order to eliminate the minute air bubbles. After this, you should use a moist cloth to clean the margins of the seal. After that, put the lids on the jars. Also, be sure to fix the bands or rings so that they close properly and there is no leaking.

- Put the jars somewhere dry and dark to store them. Please allow it to cool. Keep in the refrigerator, and consume within a week of storage.

- Relish the taste whenever you need it with the delicacy of your choice.

Calorie content: 50 kilocalories

Conserve made of cantaloupe and peaches.

Time Required for Preparation: 5 Minutes

Servings: 3-4 (½ pint) jars.

Ingredients:

- 1/4 cup almonds that have been blanched and roughly chopped
- 1 and 12 cups of chopped cantaloupe
- 1 and 12 cups of chopped peeled and sliced peaches 2 cups sugar
- ½ tbsp lemon juice
- nutmeg, ground, one-fourth teaspoon 1/8 teaspoon salt
- 1 eight-tenth of a teaspoon of grated orange rind
- Directions:
- Combine the cantaloupe and peaches in a heavy-bottomed skillet or other kind of cooking pot. Bring the mixture to a boil, and then continue cooking it for around 10 minutes. Maintain a constant stirring.
- Mix sugar and lemon juice together in a mixing bowl.
- Bring the mixture to a boil, and after it's boiling, add the rest of the ingredients while stirring.
- Bring the mixture to a boil and continue boiling until the thermometer reaches 220 degrees Fahrenheit. Continue boiling the mixture for another 10 to 12 minutes over

medium heat until it becomes firm and thick. Continuously stir the pot

- When you are finished, use a jar funnel to transfer the hot mixture into the jars that have been previously sterilized. Keep a headspace that is a quarter of an inch from the top of the jar.

- Make use of a spatula made of a material other than metal and swirl the mixture gently in order to eliminate the minute air bubbles. After this, you should use a moist cloth to clean the margins of the seal. After that, put the lids on the jars. Also, be sure to fix the bands or rings so that they close properly and there is no leaking.

- Place in a water bath for about ten to fifteen minutes.

- Put the jars somewhere dry and dark to store them. Please allow it to cool. Place in the coldest part of your refrigerator.

- Relish the taste whenever you need it with the delicacy of your choice.

117 calories per 100 grams (kcal)

A conserve made with cranberries and apples.

Time Required for Preparation: 15 Minutes

Servings: 3-4 (1/2 pint) jars.

Ingredients:

- 1 Granny Smith apple, peeled, cored, and diced into bite-sized pieces also. Orange juice and zest from one orange

- One lemon's worth of zest and juice 1 and a half cups worth of fresh cranberries 1 ¾ cups sugar

- 1/4 cup finely chopped hazelnuts, walnuts, or pecans

- ¾ cup raisins 1 ounce of water

Directions:

- Mix the water, sugar, and cranberries together in a large cooking pot or a saucepan with a deep dish.

- Bring the mixture to a boil, then reduce the heat to a simmer and cook for 5 minutes while stirring constantly. Combine the apple, juice, and zest in a mixing bowl.

- Bring the mixture to a boil and continue boiling it until the thermometer reaches 220 degrees Fahrenheit. Continue boiling the mixture for approximately 15 minutes over medium heat until it becomes firm and thick. Continuously stir the pot

- Combine the raisins and almonds in a bowl.

- When you are finished, use a jar funnel to transfer the hot mixture into the jars that have been previously sterilized. Keep a headspace that is a quarter of an inch from the top of the jar.

- Make use of a spatula made of a material other than metal and swirl the mixture gently in order to eliminate the minute air bubbles. After this, you should use a moist cloth to clean the margins of the seal. After that, put the lids on the jars. Also, be sure to fix the bands or rings so that they close properly and there is no leaking.

- Put the jars somewhere dry and dark to store them. Please allow it to cool. Keep in the refrigerator, and consume within a week of storage.

- Relish the taste whenever you need it with the delicacy of your choice.

139 calories per 100 grams.

Chapter Seven
Salsas

Relish made with corn

Time Required for Preparation: 20 Minutes

Servings: three to four pints.

Ingredients:

- 2 tablespoons mustard seeds 1/2 teaspoon turmeric

- 1/2 milligram of cumin seed, ground

- 2 big cucumbers, seeded, skinned, and coarsely diced before being used. 1 1/2 cups apple cider vinegar, 5% acidity

- 2 cups of chopped onions

- 2 cups of chopped red bell peppers that have been seeded and chopped

- 4 cups of corn kernels, plum or Roma tomatoes, sliced red or green serrano chili peppers, seeded and minced,

- 4 cups of corn kernels

- 1 and a quarter cups of sugar and a few teaspoons of kosher salt

- 1/2 milligram of ground black pepper

Directions:

- Cucumbers, onions, and red bell peppers should be pulsed: Cucumbers, onions, and bell peppers should be pulsed in a food processor no more than three or four times each batch, so that they are still distinct from one another and are not puréed. If necessary, work on each batch individually.

- Mix in the remaining components, then boil for twenty-five minutes: Put the ingredients in a heavy-bottomed saucepan of a medium size, between 4 and 6 quarts in capacity. To the bowl, add the corn, tomatoes, serrano chiles, sugar, salt, pepper, vinegar, turmeric, crushed cumin, and mustard seed. Bring the liquid to a boil. Bring the temperature down to a simmer. Cook for another 25 minutes with the cover on.

- Scoop into jars: The corn relish, once placed in clean jars and sealed, will keep for 4-6 weeks if stored in the refrigerator.

- Relish the taste whenever you need it with the delicacy of your choice.

Calorie content: 354 kilocalories

Salsa Verde.

Time Required for Preparation: 20 Minutes

Number of servings: 3 quarts

Ingredients:

- 12 tomatoes, cored, skinned, and sliced medium-sized green tomatoes 6 to 8 jalapenos, seeded and chopped to a fine consistency

- 2 big pieces of chopped red onion 1 milliliter of garlic that has been minced

- ½ cup fresh lime juice

- a half cup of fresh cilantro, chopped 1 and 12 tablespoons of cumin seed powder 1 teaspoon of oregano that has been dried Both pepper and salt

Directions:

- Get the necessary supplies ready, including your canner that uses a water bath as well as your lids and bands.

- In a large saucepan, combine the tomatoes, jalapenos, onion, and garlic, and then stir in the lime juice.

- The other ingredients should be stirred in once the pot has been brought to a boil and covered.

- Reduce the heat and simmer the mixture for five minutes, after which you should pour it into your jars, being sure to leave approximately a half an inch of headspace.

- After cleaning the rims, placing the lid on the jar, and securing it with the metal band, set the jars in the water bath canner, and then bring the water to a boil.

- After 20 minutes, take the jars from the oven and thoroughly dry them with a clean towel. Before putting these jars away for storage, let them cool for a full day on a canning rack.

- Relish the taste whenever you need it with the delicacy of your choice.

- Calorie content: 276 kilocalories

Simple Salsa.

Time Required for Preparation: 20 Minutes

Number of servings: 3 quarts

Ingredients:

- 4 cups of diced tomatoes, which have been seeded and chopped 2 cups of green chilies that have been seeded and chopped 34 cup of onions that have been chopped 12 cup of jalapeño peppers that have been seeded and chopped 4 cloves of garlic, finely chopped

- 1 teaspoon of cumin that has been ground 1 tablespoon cilantro

- 1 teaspoon of dried oregano 1 cup of white distilled vinegar 1 ½ teaspoons table salt

Directions:

- Put all of the ingredients mentioned up top into a large saucepan. Put the saucepan on the burner and bring the liquid to a full rolling boil as soon as possible while swirling it often to prevent it from burning.

- Turn the heat down just a little bit and keep the mixture at a simmer for around twenty minutes. Mixing it up often

- Spread the salsa evenly among the four jars. It is important to remember to leave a gap of approximately half an inch at the top of each jar. After putting the lids on the jars, you will put them through the canning process using the water bath technique for 15 to 25 minutes.

- Relish the taste whenever you need it with the delicacy of your choice.

225 calories per serving.

Mango Salsa.

Time Required for Preparation: 20 Minutes

Number of servings: 3 quarts

Ingredients:

- ½ cup Water

- ¼ cup Cider vinegar, 5%

- 2 tablespoons of minced ginger 1 1/2 cups of water Red bell pepper, diced

- 1/2 teaspoon a total of six cups of crushed red pepper flakes Mango, unripe, diced

- 1/2 cup Two tablespoons worth of chopped yellow onion 1 cup of finely chopped garlic. Golden caster sugar

Directions:

- Be sure to give the mangoes and the rest of the vegetables a thorough cleaning. Mangoes should be peeled before being chopped into half-inch pieces.

- Prepare the dish by dicing the red bell pepper into half-inch strips and chopping the yellow onion into small pieces. Put this into a large saucepan or a Dutch oven. Add all of the other ingredients, give it a good toss to mix everything, then heat it up over high heat.

- After you have brought the liquid to a boil, give it a thorough swirl to dissolve the sugar. Reduce the heat to medium and let the mixture around five minutes to simmer after lowering the temperature.

- After sterilizing the Mason jars, transfer the hot salsa to the jars while allowing a half an inch of headspace in each one. Pour enough of the hot liquid into it so that each jar is filled to within half an inch of its rim.

- Before placing the lids on the jars, make sure that any air bubbles have been removed. After placing the ingredients in the water bath, wait 10 minutes before processing.

- Relish the taste whenever you need it with the delicacy of your choice.

The food has 299 calories.

Pineapple and chipotle in a bowl.

Time Required for Preparation: 20 Minutes

Number of servings: 3 quarts

Ingredients:

- 4 cups of papaya, seeded
- 2 cups of pineapples, either chopped or cubed 1 Cup raisins
- Cup lemon juice
- ½ Cup lime juice
- ½ Cup pineapple juice
- a half cup of chopped Anaheim peppers
- a few tablespoons worth of chopped onions 2 teaspoons finely chopped fresh cilantro 2 teaspoons of light brown sugar

Instructions:

- Place all ten ingredients in a pot and mix well before transferring to a bowl. During this process, you will need to stir often.
- Reduce the heat to a low simmer and continue to whisk the mixture as it continues to thicken. Put the lids on the canning jars after adding the food.
- Relish the taste whenever you need it with the delicacy of your choice.

233 calories per 100 grams.

Green Salsa.

Time Required for Preparation: 20 Minutes

Servings: 3 quarts

Ingredients:

- a total of seven cups of chopped green tomatoes 3 cups of jalapenos that have been chopped
- 2 cups of finely chopped crimson onions 2 teaspoons of garlic that has been minced
- ½ Cups lime juice
- 1 and a half cups of chopped cilantro 2 teaspoons of cumin that has been ground

Directions:

- Put all of the veggies, the garlic, and the lime in a saucepan. Bring to a boil, then reduce heat to low and simmer for five minutes. Ladle the salsa into canning jars, leaving a quarter of an inch of headspace at the top.
- Relish the taste whenever you need it with the delicacy of your choice.

133 calories per 100 grams.

Tomatillo Salsa.

Time Required for Preparation: 20 Minutes

Number of servings: 2 and a half quarts.

Ingredients:

- 1 pound and a half of tomatillos, peeled, de-husked, and rinsed
- 1 to 2 medium jalapeños, stemmed (note: spiciness will depend on heat of actual peppers used)

- 12 cup of white onion that has been chopped 1 to 2 medium-sized limes, juiced
- ½ to 1 teaspoon salt
- 1/4 cup of fresh cilantro leaves, tightly packed

Directions:

- Prepare the broiler by positioning the rack so that it is about 4 inches below the heat source. Put the tomatillos and jalapenos on a baking sheet with a rim and broil them for approximately 5 minutes, or until some of the tomatillos and jalapenos have charred.

- Take the baking sheet out of the oven, carefully turn the tomatillos and peppers over with a pair of tongs, and place them back under the broiler for another four to six minutes, or until the tomatillos have developed black spots and blisters.

- After some time has passed, halved onion, cilantro, 2 tablespoons of lime juice, and a half teaspoon of salt should be combined in a food processor or blender. After removing the tomatillos from the broiler, carefully transfer the hot tomatillos, peppers, and all of the fluids from the tomatillos and peppers into the blender or food processor.

- After this, give the combination a few pulses in a food processor until it is almost smooth and there are no large bits of tomatillo left. In the event that it is required, scrape down the edges of the pan, and then, if desired, season with extra lime juice and salt.

- Because of the naturally occurring pectin in the tomatillos, the salsa will initially have a runnier consistency, but after being stored in the refrigerator for a number of hours, it will ultimately become more substantial.

- Relish the taste whenever you need it with the delicacy of your choice.

Calorie content: 180 kilocalories

Zesty Salsa.

Time Required for Preparation: 20 Minutes

Servings per recipe: 6 quarts

Ingredients:

- 10 cups of tomatoes, coarsely diced, measured out. 1 can of tomato paste (each containing 6 ounces)
- 2 and a half cups of chopped and seeded hot peppers 5 cups of diced bell peppers, seeded and chopped 5 cups of minced onions total
- ¼ cups cider vinegar three cloves of garlic, minced
- 2 tablespoons of chopped cilantro 2 tablespoons of olive oil 3 teaspoons of salt

Directions:

- In a large saucepan, combine all of the aforementioned ingredients with the exception of the tomato paste.
- Simmer until the required consistency is reached. Stir in tomato paste.
- Place hot salsa in hot jars that have been previously sterilized, allowing a head space of 1/4 inch. Perform the processing for this in a bath of hot water for ten minutes.

- Relish the taste whenever you need it with the delicacy of your choice.

142 calories per 100 grams.

Salsa made with corn and cherry tomatoes.

Time Required for Preparation: 20 Minutes

Servings per recipe: 6 quarts

Ingredients:

- 1/2 cup of fresh cilantro that has been chopped
- 1 cup of diced red onion 5 pounds of cherry tomatoes with the seeds chopped approximately
- 2 jalapenos, seeded and chopped into small pieces.
- 2 cups of corn husks and kernels (may be fresh or frozen thawed)
- ½ cup fresh lime juice (3 large or 4 medium limes) 2 teaspoons salt
- 1 teaspoon of chipotle chile powder, as an optional ingredient

Directions:

- Prepare the canner with the bubbling water. To get the containers ready for use, warm them up in the simmering water until they are. Never bring water to a boil. The tops should be washed in warm water including some soap and then set aside with the other groups.
- In a large pot made of treated steel or plated steel, bring all of the aforementioned items to a boil. Reduce

the heat and simmer for five to ten minutes while stirring the mixture occasionally.

- Place the hot salsa in a heated container, allowing a half an inch of headspace between the salsa and the lid. Get rid of all of the air bubbles. Remove any debris from the edge of the container. The top should be focused on the container. After the band has been applied, adjust it so that it is fingertip-tight. Place the container into the water canner that is bubbling. Continue doing so until each of the containers is full.

- The used jars should be processed in a water bath for fifteen minutes, although this time should be adjusted based on the altitude. After taking the jars out of the oven and turning off the heat, remove the lids and then set them aside for at least five minutes. Take the jars out of the oven and allow them to cool.

- Relish the taste whenever you need it with the delicacy of your choice.

311 calories (kcal) of nutrition

Classic Fiesta Salsa.

Time Required for Preparation: 20 Minutes

Servings: 32.

Ingredients:

- 4 and a half cups of diced tomatoes, a tablespoon of white vinegar, and four and a half cups of white

- 1/4 measuring cup of salsa

Directions:

- In the first step, put your chopped tomatoes, vinegar, and salsa of choice into a big pot and set it on the stove over medium heat.

- Bring your mixture to a boil in the saucepan. After the mixture has reached a boil, turn the heat down to a low setting, and then let it to simmer for the following five minutes.

- Take away from the heat and let it cool down completely.

- Canning jars should have their lids on tightly before the mixture is poured inside.

- For the next ten minutes, place your jars in some hot water and bring them to a boil. Take the dish out of the oven and let it rest for a few minutes before putting it in the refrigerator. When you are ready, use it whatever you choose.

- Relish the taste whenever you need it with the delicacy of your choice.

152 calories (kcal) in total.

Salsa made with fresh tomatoes.

Time Required for Preparation: 20 Minutes

Number of servings: 4 quarts

- Tomatoes, freshly sliced and measured out in pounds

- 2 huge green peppers, seeded and sliced in small pieces

- 2 big yellow onions, 1 jalapeño, seeded and sliced,

- 2 tablespoons of minced garlic
- 2 tablespoons of fresh cilantro that has been chopped.

- 1 teaspoon of chopped garlic
- 1 tablespoon of minced onion
- 1 teaspoon of canning salt
- 1/3 cup of white vinegar that has been distilled

Directions:

- Get your canner ready for a water bath as well as your jars.

- Put all of the ingredients listed above into a big pot, and then bring the mixture up to a boil. The heat should be turned down, and the salsa should be allowed to simmer for five minutes.

- Place the salsa in the jars you have prepared, being sure to leave approximately a half an inch of headspace. After sterilizing the jars, follow the instructions in the step-by-step tutorial to place them in the canner that uses a water bath.

- The jars should be processed for a total of 35 minutes, after which they should be allowed to cool as instructed in the step-by-step guidance.

- Relish the taste whenever you need it with the delicacy of your choice.

Calorie content comes in at 162

I am grateful that you are using this book. I am sincerely concerned about the quality of your experience as a customer, and I am curious about how you have evaluated the process of reading this book. Your input, whether in the form of thoughts or opinions, is very much appreciated. I would appreciate it if you could let me know whether or not you were satisfied with the experience and whether or not you have any queries that you'd like answered. Thank you.

Conclusion

It is my aim that you will now be able to save your home-cooked, nutritious meals in canning jars at any time thanks to the several methods of canning using a water bath that are presented in this cookbook, as well as the extensive collection of recipes. Canning in a water bath or under pressure is something you can do like a pro if you have all the necessary equipment and instruments. To get started, all you need are some fundamental rules and recipes that are both fundamental and useful for food preservation. Canning diverse types of food items might be challenging for novices, but with enough practice and training, anybody can become an expert in this trade.

Printed in Dunstable, United Kingdom